DICTIONARY of NEW WORDS

Published by
Lotus Press Publishers & Distributors

DICTIONARY of NEW WORDS

Sanjay Bhatt

Lotus PRESS
4735/22, Prakash Deep Building,
Ansari Road, Daryaganj,
New Delhi- 110002

Lotus Press Publishers & Distributors
Unit No.220, 2nd Floor, 4735/22, Prakash Deep Building,
Ansari Road, Daryaganj, New Delhi- 110002
Ph:- 32903912, 23280047, 098118-38000
Email : lotuspress1984@gmail.com
Visit us : www.lotuspress.co.in

Dictionary of New Words

ISBN : 978-81-8382-257-2

Printed & Published by : **Lotus Press Publishers & Distributors,** New Delhi- 2

PREFACE

Like it or not, people judge you by the words you use. Every time you speak to someone they are trying to figure out how competent, successful, and smart you are.

Research has shown that people are more likely to be judged as competent and smart when they speak with a good vocabulary.

Language and thought are inseparable. All of us need words to think and to think we need words. Language is the tool our minds use to think, plan, solve problems, and succeed.

As we learn and understand thc meaning of more words, we are able to use better descriptive words to communicate our thoughts clearly and fluently. Further, this can reduce the chances of making eliminating noises, such as 'umm', 'uhh', 'you see', 'you know', and 'I mean', while indulging in face to face conversation. It is only after learning colourful and interesting words and strengthening vocabulary that one will be able to project a more intelligent image in public and personal grounds.

Therefore, we can say that knowing more words gives our mind more ways to think about things and more tools to plan and solve problems. Having a better vocabulary literally improves your ability to think.

English language has vast vocabulary. Further, since it is a growing language, every year new words are added to it.

People, for whom English is a second language, it is hard to keep track of new words. The present book is an effort to help such people develop a rich vocabulary.

The book is a dictionary of new words. Accompanied by meaning and usage, it aims at helping the reader improve their vocabulary and use the new words they come across in correct manner.

We hope the strenuous effort of the author would be appreciated and the approach would help the readers accomplish their aim.

Author

CONTENTS

A

Abash (Verb)

Meaning: to feel ashamed, to embarrass

Use: Rashmi felt abashed by her inability to remember her lines in the school chorus of Old McDonald Had a Farm.

Abate (Verb)

Meaning: to subside, to reduce

Use: Bad weather abates when good weather begins to return.

Abdicate (Verb)

Meaning: to step down from a position of power or responsibility

Use: Even people who aren't royals can abdicate duties and responsibilities.

Aberration (Noun)

Meaning: something not typical, a deviation from the standard

Use: The chef at this restaurant is dreadful. The good meal we just had was an aberration.

Abhor (Verb)

Meaning: to hate very, very much; to detest

Use: Hating a person is almost friendly in comparison with abhorring him or her.

Abject (Adjective)

Meaning: hopeless; extremely sad and servile, defeated, utterly bummed out

Use: An abject person is one who is crushed and without hope.

Abnegate (Verb)

Meaning: to deny oneself things, to reject, to renounce

Use: Self-abnegation is giving up oneself, usually for some higher cause.

Abridge (Verb)

Meaning: to shorten, to condense

Use: The thoughtful editor had abridged the massive book by removing the boring parts.

Abortive (Adjective)

Meaning: unsuccessful

Use: Mary and Elizabeth made an abortive effort to bake a birthday cake, which evidently tasted nothing like a cake!

Absolute (Adjective)

Meaning: total, unlimited, perfect

Use: An absolute ruler is one who is ruled by no one else.

Absolve (Verb)

Meaning: to forgive or free from blame, to free from sin, to free from an obligation.

Use: The priest absolved the sinner who had come to church to confess his sin.

Abstinent (Adjective)

Meaning: abstaining, voluntarily not doing something, especially something pleasant that is bad for you or has a bad reputation

Use: Sonakshi, who was dieting, tried to be abstinent, but when she saw the chocolate cake she realised that she would probably have to eat the entire thing.

Abstract (Adjective)

Meaning: theoretical, impersonal

Use: To like something in the abstract is to like the idea of it.

Acrimonious (Adjective)

Meaning: full of spite, bitter, nasty

Use: Relations between the competing candidates were so acrimonious that each refused to acknowledge the presence of the other.

Acrid (Adjective)

Meaning: harsh, like acid

Use: The drinks we had at the party had an acrid taste. It was harsh and unpleasant.

Acumen (Noun)

Meaning: keenness of judgement, mental sharpness

Use: A man who knows how to turn a dollar into a million dollars overnight might be said to have a lot of business acumen.

Acute (Adjective)

Meaning: sharp, shrewd

Use: If your eyesight is acute, you can see things that other people can't.

Adage (Noun)

Meaning: an old saying, a familiar bit of wisdom

Use: He wants to live by the adage – Live and Let Live.

Adamant (Adjective)

Meaning: stubborn, unyielding, completely inflexible

Use: A very hard substance, like a diamond, is also adamant.

Adherent (Noun)

Meaning: follower, supporter, believer

Use: There are innumerable adherents to causes, ideas, philosophies, and a lot, to religion.

Address (Verb)

Meaning: to speak, to direct one's attention to a problem to face it and set about solving it.

Use: Rohit addressed the problem of addressing the convention by sitting down and writing his speech.

Admonish (Verb)

Meaning: to scold gently, to warn

Use: The boys' mother admonished them not to eat the pie that she had just baked.

Adroit (Adjective)

Meaning: skilful, dexterous, clever, shrewd, socially at ease

Use: Right-handed people are thought to be more dexterous and adroit than left-handed people.

Adulation (Noun)

Meaning: wild or excessive admiration, flattery

Use: The rock star grew to abhor the adulation of his fans.

Adulterate (Verb)

Meaning: to contaminate, to make impure

Use: Vegetarians do not like their foods adulterated with animal fats.

Aesthetic (Adjective)

Meaning: having to do with artistic beauty, artistic

Use: Our art professor has a highly developed aesthetic sense. He found things to admire in paintings that, to us, looked like garbage.

Adverse (Adjective)

Meaning: unfavourable, antagonistic

Use: Airplanes often don't fly in adverse weather.

Affable (Adjective)

Meaning: easy to talk to, friendly

Use: Suhana is an affable girl; she can strike up a pleasant conversation with almost anyone.

Affectation (Noun)

Meaning: unnatural or artificial behaviour, usually intended to impress

Use: Shruti had somehow acquired the absurd affectation of pretending that she didn't know how to turn on a television set.

Affinity (Noun)

Meaning: sympathy, attraction, kinship, similarity

Use: Children have an affinity for trouble. That is, they offer to find themselves in it.

Affluent (Adjective)

Meaning: rich, prosperous

Use: A person can be affluent; all it takes is money.

Agenda (Noun)

Meaning: programme, the things to be done

Use: A person who has sneaky ambitions or plans is often said to have a secret or hidden agenda.

Agrarian (Adjective)

Meaning: relating to land, relating to the management or farming of land

Use: Agrarian usually has to do with farming. Think of agriculture. Politics in this country often pit the rural, agrarian interests against the urban interests.

Aggregate (Noun)

Meaning: sum total, a collection of separate things mixed together

Use: The teacher wanted to know aggregate marks of all the students.

Agnostic (Noun)

Meaning: one who believes that the existence of a God can be neither proved nor disproved

Use: Rohan is an agnostic.

Alacrity (Noun)

Meaning: cheerful eagerness or readiness to respond

Use: David could hardly wait for his parents to leave; he carried their luggage out to the car with great alacrity.

Allege (Verb)

Meaning: to assert without proof

Use: The police have alleged that he or she committed the crime, but a jury hasn't made a decision yet.

Allocate (Verb)

Meaning: to distribute, to assign, to allot

Use: The office manager had allocated just seven paper clips for our entire department.

Alleviate (Adjective)

Meaning: to relieve, usually temporarily or in-completely, to make bearable, to lessen

Use: Visiting the charming pet cemetery alleviated the women's grief over the death of her canary.

Alloy (Noun)

Meaning: a combination of two or more things, usually metals

Use: Brass is an alloy of copper and zinc. That is, you make brass by combining copper and zinc.

Allusion (Noun)

Meaning: an indirect reference (often to a literary work), a hint

Use: In today's world, comic books have become reference points in many ways. Everyone understands a Superman allusion or a Batman joke.

Aloof (Adjective)

Meaning: uninvolved, standing off, keeping one's distance

Use: Cats are often said to be aloof because they usually mind their own business and don't crave the affection of people.

Altruism (Noun)

Meaning: selflessness, generosity, devotion to the interests of others

Use: The private foundation depended on the altruism of the extremely rich old man.

Ambiguous (Adjective)

Meaning: unclear in meaning, confusing, capable of being interpreted in different ways

Use: The poem we read in English class was ambiguous. No one had any idea what the poet was trying to say.

Ambivalent (Adjective)

Meaning: undecided, neutral

Use: He was ambivalent to the argument between his mother and wife and left the place for the night.

Ameliorate (Verb)

Meaning: to make better or more tolerable

Use: The condition of the prisoners was ameliorated when the warden gave them colour television sets and keys to their cells.

Amenable (Adjective)

Meaning: obedient; willing to give in to the wishes of another, agreeable

Use: The plumber was amenable to paying my bill with jelly beans, which was lucky, because I had more jelly beans than money.

Amenity (Adjective)

Meaning: pleasantness, attractive or comfortable feature

Use: The amenities at the local club include a swimming pool, a golf course and a fallout shelter.

Abstruse (Adjective)

Meaning: hard to understand

Use: Nuclear physics is a subject that is too abstruse for most people.

Abysmal (Adjective)

Meaning: extremely hopeless or wretched, bottomless

Use: Abysmal despair is despair so deep that no hope seems possible.

Accolade (Noun)

Meaning: an award, an honour

Use: The dancing troupe received accolades for its performance.

Accost (Verb)

Meaning: to approach and speak to someone

Use: Juhi chopped the stranger who accosted her in the street and was embarrassed to find he was an old blind man.

Acerbic (Adjective)

Meaning: bitter, sour or astringent in taste

Use: Sohan sat silently as our teacher read aloud her acerbic comments on his paper.

Acquiesce (Verb)

Meaning: to comply passively, to accept, to assent, to agree

Use: The pirates asked Pete to walk the plank. He took one look at their swords and then acquiesced.

Amnesty (Noun)

Meaning: an official pardon for a group of people who have violated a law or policy

Use: When a state government declares a tax amnesty, it is saying that if people pay the taxes they owe, the government will officially forget that they broke the law by not paying them in the first place.

Amiable (Adjective)

Meaning: friendly, agreeable

Use: Our amiable guide made us feel right at home in what would otherwise have been a cold and forbidding museum.

Amoral (Adjective)

Meaning: lacking a sense of right and wrong, neither good nor bad, neither moral nor immoral

Use: Very young children are amoral. When they cry, they aren't being bad or good; they're merely doing what they have to do.

Amorous (Adjective)

Meaning: felling loving, especially in a sexual sense in love, relating to love

Use: The amorous couple made quite a scene at the movie. The movie they were watching, Love Story, was pretty amorous itself.

Amorphous (Adjective)

Meaning: shapeless, without a regular or stable shape, bloodlike

Use: Abhijeet's teacher said that his term paper was amorphous. She said that it was as shapeless and disorganised as a cloud.

Anachronism (Noun)

Meaning: something out of place in time or history, an incongruity

Use: In this day of impersonal hospitals, a family doctor who will wait you at home seems like an anachronism.

Anarchy (Noun)

Meaning: absence of government or control, lawlessness, disorder

Use: The country fell into a state of anarchy after the rebels kidnapped the president and locked the legislature inside the Assembly House.

Anecdote (Noun)

Meaning: a short account of a humorous or revealing incident

Use: The old lady kept the motorcycle gang thoroughly amused with anecdote after anecdote about her cute little dog.

Anguish (Noun)

Meaning: agonising physical or mental pain

Use: There had been a nurse in the emergency room for twenty years but she had never gotten used to the anguish of accident victims.

Animosity (Noun)

Meaning: resentment, hostility, ill will

Use: A person whose look could kill is a person whose animosity is evident.

Anomaly (Noun)

Meaning: an aberration, an irregularity, a deviation

Use: A snowy winter day is not an anomaly, but a snowy July day is.

Antecedent (Noun)

Meaning: someone or something that went before, something that provides a model for something that came after it

Use: The horse-drawn wagon is an antecedent of the modern automobile.

Antipathy (Noun)

Meaning: from dislike; a dislike

Use: I feel antipathy toward bananas wrapped in ham. I do not want them for dinner.

Antithesis (Noun)

Meaning: the direct opposite

Use: Seeta is the antithesis of Geeta. Seeta is bright and beautiful. Geeta is dull and plain.

Apartheid (Noun)

Meaning: the abhorrent policy of racial segregation and oppression in the Republic of South Africa

Use: Critics have sometimes accused American public schools of practicing educational apartheid, by providing substandard schooling for nonwhites.

Apathy (Noun) (Check this)

Meaning: lack of interest, lack of feeling

Use: People have shown surprising apathy toward important social problems.

Aphorism (Noun)

Meaning: a brief, often witty saying, a proverb

Use: Benjamin Franklin was fond of aphorisms. He was frequently aphoristic.

Apocalypse (Noun)

Meaning: a prophetic revelation, especially one concerning the end of the world

Use: The destruction of the ozone layer and the spread of fast-food restaurants to every corner of the universe. To make such predictions or to be deeply pessimistic is to be apocalyptic.

Apocryphal (Noun)

Meaning: of dubious authenticity, fictitious, spurious

Use: An apocryphal story is one whose truth is not proven or whose falsehood is strongly suspected.

Apotheosis (Noun)

Meaning: elevation to divine status, the perfect example of something

Use: George is unbearable to be with. He thinks he's the apotheosis of masculinity.

Appease (Verb)

Meaning: to soothe, to pacify by giving in to

Use: Rahul appeased his angry mother by promising to make his bed every morning without fail until the end of time.

Appreciate (Noun)

Meaning: to increase in value

Use: The Harsh bought their house twenty years ago for one lakh rupees, but it has appreciated considerably since then.

Apprehensive (Adjective)

Meaning: worried, anxious

Use: The apprehensive child clung to his father's leg as the two of them walked into the main circus tent to watch the lion tamer.

Approbation (Noun)

Meaning: approval, praise

Use: The ambassador's actions met with the approbation of his commander-in-chief.

Appropriate (Verb)

Meaning: to take without permission, to set aside for a particular use

Use: The deer and raccoons appropriated the vegetables in our garden last summer. This year we'll build a better fence.

Aptitude (Noun)

Meaning: capacity for learning, natural ability

Use: I tried to repair my car but as I sat on the floor of my garage surrounded by mysterious parts, I realised that I had no aptitude for automobile repair.

Arbiter (Noun)

Meaning: one who decides, a judge

Use: A judge is an arbiter.

Arbitrary (Adjective)

Meaning: random, capricious

Use: The old judge was arbitrary in sentencing criminals; there was no sensible pattern to the sentences he handed down.

Arcane (Adjective)

Meaning: mysterious, known only to a select few

Use: We could make out only a little of the arcane inscription on the old trunk.

Archaic (Adjective)

Meaning: extremely old, ancient; outdated

Use: Archaic civilizations are ones that disappeared a long time ago.

Archetype (Noun)

Meaning: an original model or pattern

Use: Plato is the archetype of all philosophers.

Ardent (Adjective)

Meaning: passionate

Use: Rehana happily stuffed badgers from morning to night. She was an ardent taxidermist.

Arduous (Adjective)

Meaning: hard, difficult

Use: The arduous care trip was made even more difficult by the fact that all four tires went flat, one after another.

Aristocratic (Adjective)

Meaning: of noble birth, snobbish

Use: Prince Charles is aristocratic. He is member of the British aristocracy.

Artful (Adjective)

Meaning: Crafty, wily, sly

Use: After dinner, the artful counsellor told the campers that there was a madman loose in the woods, thus causing them to lie quietly in the tent.

Artifice (Noun)

Meaning: a clever trick; cunning

Use: The Trojan Horse was an artifice designed to get the soldiers inside the walls.

Ascetic (Adjective)

Meaning: hermitlike, practicing self-denial

Use: In his effort to save money, Roy led an ascetic existence. He never went out, he never ate anything but soup and he never had any fun.

Assiduous (Adjective)

Meaning: hardworking, quite diligent

Use: Abhishek was the only assiduous student in the entire math class. All the other students had to copy their homework from him.

Assimilate (Verb)

Meaning: to take in, to absorb, to learn thoroughly

Use: Your body assimilates nutrients from the food you eat.

Assuage (Verb)

Meaning: to soothe, to pacify, to ease the pain of, to relieve

Use: Bhuvesh was extremely angry, but his brother assuaged him by promising to leave the house and never return.

Astute (Adjective)

Meaning: shrewd, keen in judgement

Use: Anand, who notices everything that is important and many things that other people don't see, is an astute observer.

Audacity (Noun)

Meaning: boldness, reckless daring, impertinence

Use: Sharavan had the audacity to suggest that it was all her fault.

Augment (Verb)

Meaning: to make bigger, to add or to increase

Use: The army augmented its attack by sending in a few thousand more soldiers.

Auspicious (Adjective)

Meaning: favourable, promising, pointing to a good result

Use: A clear sky in the morning is an auspicious sign on the day of a picnic.

Austere (Adjective)

Meaning: unadorned, stern, forbidding, without excess

Use: The Malhotra's house was very austere. There was no furniture in it and there was nothing hanging on the walls.

Autocratic (Adjective)

Meaning: ruling with absolute authority, extremely bossy

Use: A two-year-old can be very autocratic–it wants what it wants when it wants it.

Autonomous (Adjective)

Meaning: acting independently

Use: An autonomous nation is one that is independent–it governs itself. It is said to have autonomy.

Avarice (Noun)

Meaning: greed, excessive love of riches

Use: The rich man's avarice was annoying to everyone who wanted to lay hands on some of his money.

Avuncular (Adjective)

Meaning: like an uncle, especially a nice uncle

Use: Pratibha likes her neighbour, Mr. Sharma, for his avuncular attitude towards her.

Awry (Adjective)

Meaning: off course, twisted to one side

Use: The hunter's bullet went awry. Instead of hitting the bear, it hit an-other hunter.

Axiom (Noun)

Meaning: a self-evident rule or truth, a widely accepted saying

Use: Everything that is living dies is an axiom.

B

Babbler (Verb)

Meaning: to talk half articulately

Use: Shruti could not understand what Dheeraj wanted to say, simply because he is such a babbler.

Backbone (Noun)

Meaning: spine, chief support of anything

Use: Mr. Gautam had to mend his ways to keep Raghu from leaving the office; he serves like the backbone of the company.

Ballast (Noun)

Meaning: heavy material kept in ship's hold to keep it steady

Use: My work is to keep the ship steady by using ballast.

Balloonist (Noun)

Meaning: one who flies in balloon

Use: I am hiring a balloonist for my party decoration.

Bandit (Noun)

Meaning: lawless robber

Use: Robin Hood is a very popular Bandit.

Bankrupt (Adjective)

Meaning: person who is unable to pay his debts

Use: The company went bankrupt, but the CEO kept his private jet.

Banal (Adjective)

Meaning: original, ordinary

Use: The dinner conversation was so banal that Aradhna fell asleep in her dessert dish.

Bane (Noun)

Meaning: poison, torment, cause of harm

Use: The criminal used bane to take his revenge on the police informant.

Bastion (Noun)

Meaning: stronghold, fortress, fortified place

Use: The robbers terrorised the village for several weeks and then escaped to their bastion high in the treacherous mountains.

Beam (Noun)

Meaning: long piece of timber of iron

Use: There is a high beam resolution of the light emitted from the crystal torch.

Beard (Noun)

Meaning: hairs that grow on cheek and chin

Use: The old man was crouching forward, lapping milk from the great bowl, his beard dripping.

Beaten (Adjective)

Meaning: thinned by hammering

Use: Arun used to be a jolly man, but now he looks like beaten by circumstances.

Beatific (Adjective)

Meaning: making blessed

Use: The bride had a beatific smile on her face as she walked down the aisle.

Bedew (Verb)

Meaning: to make moist

Use: Falling tears make his face bedew.

Beetle (Noun)

Meaning: insect with horny wing-covers

Use: They saw many beetles in the garden.

Befit (Verb)

Meaning: to be suitable

Use: At all events, you ought to thank your parents for it, it is for your benefit it is made.

Befool (Verb)

Meaning: to make fool of

Use: The immigrant was duped because he befooled everyone.

Beg (Verb)

Meaning: to ask for alms

Use: The old man was so poor that he had to beg in the street.

Beget (Verb)

Meaning: to give birth to, to create, to lead, to cause

Use: Those who lie should be creative and have good memories, since one lie leads often to another lie, which begets another.

Beggar (Noun)

Meaning: one who begs

Use: The beggar asked money for food.

Beguile (Noun)

Meaning: to deceive

Use: He beguiled the time with gardening.

Behest (Noun)

Meaning: command

Use: I called the office at the behest of my assistant.

Belief (Noun)

Meaning: faith, trust

Use: My belief in you is as strong as ever.

Bellow (Verb)

Meaning: to roar

Use: The headmaster bellowed at the children.

Belong (Verb)

Meaning: to be property of

Use: This toy belongs to my daughter.

Beloved (Adjective)

Meaning: much loved

Use: My beloved left me for another girl.

Belabor (Verb)

Meaning: to go over repeatedly or to an absurd extent

Use: Mr. Ishwar spent the entire period belabouring the obvious. He made the same dumb observation over and over again.

Beleaguer (Verb)

Meaning: to surround, to besiege, to harass

Use: No one could leave the beleaguered city; the attacking army had closed off all the exits.

Belie (Verb)

Meaning: to give a false impression of, to contradict

Use: The messy appearance of the banquet table belied the huge effort that had gone into setting it up.

Belittle (Verb)

Meaning: to make to seem little, to put someone down

Use: The chairman's belittling comments made everyone feel small.

Belligerent (Adjective)

Meaning: combative, quarrelsome, waging war

Use: Ali was so belligerent that the convention had the feel of a boxing match.

Bemused (Adjective)

Meaning: confused, bewildered

Use: Rohan was bemused when all the lights and appliances in his house began switching on add off for no apparent reason.

Bend (Verb)

Meaning: to curve

Use: A bend in the road.

Beneath (Adjective)

Meaning: under, below

Use: They watched the boat breaking up on the rocks beneath.

Benefactor (Noun)

Meaning: one who provides help, especially in the form of a gift or donation

Use: Rohan is the benefactor of his father's policy.

Benevolent (Adjective)

Meaning: generous, kind, doing good deeds

Use: Giving money to the poor is a benevolent act.

Benign (Adjective)

Meaning: gentle, not harmful, kind, mild

Use: Bhumika has benign personality. She is not at all unpleasant to be with.

Bequest (Noun)

Meaning: something left to some in a will

Use: If your next-door neighbour leaves you all his wealth in a will, the money is a bequest from him to you. It is not polite to request a bequest. Just keep smiling and hope for the best.

Bequeath (Verb)

Meaning: to leave property by will

Use: She bequeathed her art collection to the town.

Bereaved (Adjective)

Meaning: deprived or left desolate especially through death, bereaved means the same thing as bereft

Use: The children were bereaved by the death of their pet. Then they got a new pet.

Berth (Noun)

Meaning: sleeping room in ship

Use: A comfortable berth as head of the department.

Beryl (Noun)

Meaning: pale green precious stone

Use: An astrologer suggested me to use Beryl for my business.

Beseem (Verb)

Meaning: to suit, to befit

Use: This kind of behaviour does not beseem a young woman.

Beset (Verb)

Meaning: to harass; to surround

Use: The bereft widow was beset by grief.

Besides (Adverb)

Meaning: in addition to

Use: No one besides the owner could control that dog.

Besom (Noun)

Meaning: long – handled broom

Use: The witch used a besom to fly over the town.

Bestir (Verb)

Meaning: to rouse into action

Use: After a heated argument, Ravi bestirred himself to look for work.

Better (Noun)

Meaning: one who bets

Use: I am better in Math than English.

Betake (Verb)

Meaning: to move or go to a place

Use: He betake it first than others.

Betel (Noun)

Meaning: climbing plant of which leaves are chewed

Use: Southeast Asians chew dried leaves of pepper plant with betel nut.

Betide (Verb)

Meaning: to happen

Use: "What has betided my children?" he asked angrily when he saw the babysitter roaming carelessly around the house and the children shying away from him.

Betrothal (Noun)

Meaning: marriage agreement

Use: Nisha's betrothal was secret.

Betray (Verb)

Meaning: to disclose or deliver by treachery

Use: Her pale face betrayed her fear.

Blasphemy (Noun)

Meaning: irreverence; an insult to something held sacred; profanity

Use: A person who says insulting things is blasphemous.

Blatant (Adjective)

Meaning: unpleasantly or offensively noisy; glaring

Use: Dinesh was blatantly critical of our efforts. That is, he was noisy and obnoxious in making his criticisms.

Blight (Noun)

Meaning: a disease in plants; anything that injures or destroys

Use: An early frost proved blight to the citrus crops last year, so we had no orange juice for breakfast.

Blithe (Adjective)

Meaning: carefree; cheerful

Use: The blither birds in the garden were making so much noise that Paul began to think about the shotgun in the attic.

Bourgeois (Adjective)

Meaning: middle class, usually in a pejorative sense; boringly conventional

Use: A hip young city dweller might reject life in the suburbs as being too bourgeois.

Bovine (Adjective)

Meaning: cow related; cow like

Use: Cows are bovine.

Brevity (Noun)

Meaning: briefness

Use: The audience was deeply grateful for the brevity of the after dinner speaker's remarks.

Broach (Verb)

Meaning: to open up a subject for discussion, Often a delicate subject

Use: Heena was proud of her new dress, so no one knows how to broach the subject with here of how silly grandmothers look in leather.

Bucolic (Adjective)

Meaning: charmingly rural; rustic; country like

Use: The bucolic scene didn't do much for the city child, who preferred screaming fire engines and honking horns to the sound of a babbling brook.

Burgeon (Verb)

Meaning: to expand; to flourish

Use: The burgeoning weeds in our yard soon overwhelmed the grass.

Burlesque (Noun)

Meaning: a ludicrous, mocking, or exaggerated imitation

Use: Vaudeville actors frequently performed burlesque works on the stage.

Bevel (Noun)

Meaning: instrument for measuring angles

Use: A chisel has a bevel on its cutting edge.

Beverage (Noun)

Meaning: drink, liquor

Use: Last night, I tasted different kind of beverage.

Bewitch (Verb)

Meaning: to put spell on

Use: She bewitched us with her smile.

Bewail (Verb)

Meaning: to lament over

Use: All your songs seem to bewail dissatisfaction in love.

Beyond (Adjective)

Meaning: at farther side of

Use: My house is just beyond those trees.

Blunder (Noun)

Meaning: gross mistake

Use: He blundered into a situation he knew nothing about it.

Blunt (Adjective)

Meaning: not sharp

Use: This knife has been blunted by years of use.

Blush (Noun)

Meaning: redness of face

Use: That girl blushes easily.

Bluster (Verb)

Meaning: to talk in noisy manner

Use: He was still blustering, but there was panic in his eyes.

Board (Noun)

Meaning: stripe of wood

Use: He wrote a few more notes on the display board.

Botany (Noun)

Meaning: science of plant life

Use: I spent my most of time in botany class.

Bracelet (Noun)

Meaning: ornament for wrist

Use: I put on the gold bracelet which he had given to me.

Burglary (Noun)

Meaning: crime of house breaking

Use: He has been arrested for burglary.

Buy (Verb)

Meaning: to purchase

Use: Certainly there are lots of things in life that money won't buy.

C

Cacophony (Noun)

Meaning: harsh-sounding mixture of words, voices, or sounds

Use: A lot of people all shouting at once would produce a cacophony.

Cadence (Noun)

Meaning: rhythm; the rise and fall of sounds

Use: The line of kids danced in rapid cadence.

Cajole (Noun)

Meaning: to persuade someone to do something he or she doesn't want to do

Use: I didn't want to give the speech, but Jay cajoled me into doing it by telling me what a good speaker I am. As it turned out, he simply hadn't been able to find anyone else.

Callow (Adjective)

Meaning: immature

Use: A teenager might show callow disregard for the feelings of adults.

Candor (Noun)

Meaning: truthfulness; sincere honesty

Use: My best friend exhibited candor when he told me that for many years now he has believed me to be a jerk.

Capitalism (Noun)

Meaning: free enterprise; an economic system in which businesses are owned by private citizens (not by the government) and in which the resulting products and services are sold with relatively little government control

Use: The American economy is capitalistic.

Capricious (Adjective)

Meaning: unpredictable; likely to change at any moment

Use: The weather is often said to be capricious. One minute it's snowing, the next minute it's 120 degree in the shade.

Caricature (Noun)

Meaning: a portrait or description that is purposely distorted or exaggerated, often to prove some point about its subject

Use: A caricature uses exaggeration to bring out the hidden character of its subject.

Castigate (Verb)

Meaning: to criticize severely, to chastize

Use: Jimmy's mother-in-law castigated him for forgetting to pick her up at the airport.

Catalyst (Noun)

Meaning: in chemistry, something that changes the rate of a chemical reaction without itself being changed; anything that makes something happen without being directly involved in it

Use: When the mad scientist dropped a few grains of the catalysts into his test tube, the bubbling liquid began to boil furiously.

Categorical (Adjective)

Meaning: unconditional; absolute

Use: Crooked politicians often make categorical denials of various charges against them. Then they go to jail.

Catharsis (Noun)

Meaning: purification that brings emotional relief or renewal

Use: Young Reddy swallowed the contents of a bottle of shoe polish, so his mother gave him a raw egg as a cathartic to make him vomit.

Catholic (Adjective)

Meaning: universal; embracing everything

Use: Leonardo Da Vinci was a catholic genius who excelled at everything he did.

Caustic (Adjective)

Meaning: like acid; corrosive

Use: Paint remover is a caustic substance, if you spill on your skin, your skin will burn.

Celibacy (Noun)

Meaning: abstinence from sex

Use: Celibacy is one of the requirements for gurukul student.

Censure (Verb)

Meaning: to condemn severely for doing something bad

Use: The House sometimes censures members for breaking laws or engaging in behaviour unbecoming to an elected official.

Cerebral (Adjective)

Meaning: brainy; intellectually refined

Use: A cerebral discussion is one that is filled with big words and concerns abstruse matters that ordinary people can't understand.

Chagrin (Noun)

Meaning: humiliation; embarrassed disappointment

Use: Much to my chagrin, I began to giggle during the existentialism of the outfield

Charisma (Noun)

Meaning: a magical-seeming ability to attract followers or inspire loyalty

Use: The glamorous presidential candidate had a lot of charisma. Voters didn't seem to support him as much as be entranced by him.

Charlatan (Noun)

Meaning: fraud; quack; con man

Use: The flea market usually attracts a lot of charlatans, who sell phony products that don't do what they claim they will.

Chasm (Noun)

Meaning: a deep, gaping hold; a gorge

Use: The bad guys were gaining, so the hero grabbed the heroine and swung across the chasm on a slender vine.

Chastise (Verb)

Meaning: to inflict punishment on; to discipline

Use: Mother chastised us for firing out bottle rockets through the living room window.

Chicanery (Noun)

Meaning: trickery; deceitfulness; artifice, especially legal or political

Use: Political news would be dull were it not for the chicanery of our elected officials.

Chimera (Noun)

Meaning: an illusion; a foolish fancy

Use: Susan's dream of becoming a movie star was just a chimera.

Choleric (Adjective)

Meaning: hot-tempered; quick to anger

Use: When the grumpy old man was in one of his choleric moods, the children refused to go near him.

Chronic (Adjective)

Meaning: constant; lasting a long time; inveterate

Use: Someone who always comes in last could be called a chronic loser.

Chronicle (Noun)

Meaning: a record of events in order of time; a history

Use: Sara's diary provided her mother with a detailed chronicle of her daughter's extracurricular activities.

Circuitous (Adjective)

Meaning: roundabout; not following a direct path

Use: The salesman's route was circuitous. It would go aimlessly through many small towns.

Circumlocution (Noun)

Meaning: an indirect expression; use of wordy or evasive language

Use: The lawyer's circumlocution left everyone in the courtroom wondering what had been said.

Circumscribe (Verb)

Meaning: to draw line around; to set the limits; to define; to restrict

Use: The Constitution clearly circumscribes the restrictions that can be placed on our personal freedoms.

Circumspect (Adjective)

Meaning: cautious

Use: As a public speaker, Nikhil was extremely circumspect. He always took great care not to say the wrong thing or give offense.

Circumvent (Verb)

Meaning: to frustrate as though by surrounding

Use: The angry school board circumvented the students' effort to install colour television sets in every classroom.

Civil (Adjective)

Meaning: polite; civilized; courteous

Use: Our dinner guests conducted themselves civilly when we told them we weren't going to serve them dinner after all.

Clandestine (Adjective)

Meaning: secret; sneaky; concealed and, usually, up to no good

Use: Crimes are usually clandestine, because criminals usually don't want to get caught.

Clemency (Noun)

Meaning: mercy; forgiveness; mildness

Use: The principal displayed clemency in giving the student only mild punishment for insulting the math teacher in front of the class.

Clique (Noun)

Meaning: an exclusive group bound together by some shared quality or interest

Use: The high school newspaper staff was a real clique.

Coalesce (Verb)

Meaning: to come together as one; to fuse; to unite

Use: The people in our neighbourhood coalesced into a powerful force for change in the community.

Coerce (Verb)

Meaning: to force someone to do or not to do something

Use: He was coerced into agreeing with the rest.

Cogent (Adjective)

Meaning: powerfully convincing

Use: The lawyer's argument in his client's behalf was not cogent, so the jury convicted his client.

Cognitive (Adjective)

Meaning: dealing with how we know the world around us through our senses; mental

Use: Scientists study the cognitive apparatus of human beings to pattern how computers should gather information about the world.

Cognition (Adjective)

Meaning: aware; conscious

Use: Arjun was cognizant of the dangers of sword swallowing, but he tried it anyway and hurt himself quite badly.

Coherent (Adjective)

Meaning: holding together; making sense

Use: A coherent wad of cotton balls is one that holds together.

Colloquial (Adjective)

Meaning: conversational; informal in languages

Use: A writer with a colloquial style is a writer who uses ordinary words and whose writing seems as informal as common speech.

Collusion (Noun)

Meaning: conspiracy; secret cooperation

Use: If the baseball owners were in collusion, then you could say that they had colluded.

Commensurate (Adjective)

Meaning: equal; proportionate

Use: Nitin's salary is commensurate with his abilities. Like his abilities, his salary is small.

Compelling (Adjective)

Meaning: forceful; causing to yield

Use: The recruiter's speech was so compelling that nearly everyone in the auditorium enlisted in the army when it was over.

Complement (Adverb)

Meaning: to complete or fill up; to be the perfect counterpart

Use: The flower arrangement complemented the table decorations.

Complacent (Adjective)

Meaning: self-satisfied; overly pleased with oneself; contented to a fault

Use: The football team won so many games that it became complacent and the worst team in the league snuck up and beat it.

Complicity (Noun)

Meaning: participation in wrongdoing; the act of being an accomplice

Use: Complicity among the students made it impossible to find out which of them had set fire to the English teacher.

Comprehensive (Adjective)

Meaning: covering or including everything

Use: The insurance policy was comprehensive. It covered all possible losses.

Comprise (Verb)

Meaning: to consist of

Use: A football team comprises eleven players on offense and eleven players on defence.

Conciliatory (Adjective)

Meaning: making peace, attempting to resolve a dispute through goodwill

Use: The warring countries were conciliatory at the treaty conference.

Concise (Adjective)

Meaning: brief and to the point; succinct

Use: The scientist's explanation was concise. It was brief and it helped us understand the difficult concept.

Concord (Noun)

Meaning: harmony; agreement

Use: Nations that live in concord are nations that live together in peace.

Concurrent (Adjective)

Meaning: happening at the same time; parallel

Use: The criminal was sentenced to two concurrent fifteen-year sentences.

Condescend (Verb)

Meaning: to stoop to someone else's level, usually in an offensive way; to patronize

Use: I was surprised that the president of the company had condescended to talk with me, a mere temporary employee.

Condone (Adverb)

Meaning: to overlook; to permit to happen

Use: The Principal condoned the hood's smoking in the bathroom. He simply ignored it.

Conducive (Adjective)

Meaning: promoting

Use: The chairs in the library are conducive to sleep. If you sit in them to study, you will fall asleep.

Confluence (Noun)

Meaning: a flowing together, especially of rivers; the place where they begin to flow together

Use: The confluence of the Missouri and Mississippi rivers is at St. Louis. That's the place where they join together.

Congenial (Adjective)

Meaning: agreeably suitable; pleasant

Use: The new restaurant has a congenial atmosphere. We enjoy just sitting there playing with the ice in our water glasses.

Congenital (Adjective)

Meaning: a trait or condition acquired between conception and birth: innate

Use: A congenital birth defect is one that is present at birth but was not caused by one's genes.

Conjecture (Verb)

Meaning: to goes; to deduce or infer on slight evidence

Use: If forced to conjecture, I would say the volcano will erupt in twenty-four hours.

Conjure (Verb)

Meaning: to summon or bring into being as if by magic

Use: The chef conjured (or conjured up) a fabulous gourmet meal using nothing more than the meager ingredients in Lucy's kitchen.

Connoisseur (Noun)

Meaning: an expert, particularly in matters of art or taste

Use: The artist's work was very popular, but connoisseurs rejected it as amateurish.

Consecrate (Verb)

Meaning: to make or declare sacred

Use: The priest consecrated the building by sprinkling holy water on it.

Consensus (Noun)

Meaning: unanimity or general agreement

Use: When there is a consensus, everybody feels the same way.

Consonant (Adjective)

Meaning: harmonious; in agreement

Use: The decision to construct a new gymnasium was consonant with the superintendent's belief in physical education.

Construe (Verb)

Meaning: to interpret

Use: Mohit construed his contract as giving him the right to do anything he wanted.

Consummate (Adjective)

Meaning: perfect; complete; supremely skilful

Use: A consummate pianist is an extremely good one. Nothing is lacking from the way he or she plays.

Contentious (Adjective)

Meaning: argumentative; quarrelsome

Use: A person looking for a fight is contentious.

Contiguous (Adjective)

Meaning: side by side; adjoining

Use: If two countries are contiguous, the territory they cover is continuous.

Contingent (Adjective)

Meaning: dependent; possible

Use: The people of the town were prepared for any contingent emergency. They had appointed men at the gates to stop the enemy kingdom's army.

Contrite (Adjective)

Meaning: admitting guilt; especially feeling remorseful

Use: A criminal who won't confess his crime is not contrite.

Conventional (Adjective)

Meaning: common, customary, unexceptional

Use: The architect's conventional designs did not win him awards for originality.

Convivial (Adjective)

Meaning: fond of partying; festive

Use: A convivial gathering is one in which the people present enjoy eating drinking and being together.

Copious (Adjective)

Meaning: abundant; plentiful

Use: The champagne at the wedding reception was copious but not very good.

Corollary (Noun)

Meaning: something that follows; natural consequence

Use: In Mathematics, a corollary is a law that can be deduced without further proof from a law that has already been proved.

Corroborate (Verb)

Meaning: to confirm; to back up with evidence. I knew my statement was correct when my colleague corroborated it

Use: The police could find no evidence of theft and thus could not corroborate Bill's claim that he had been robbed.

Cosmopolitan (Adjective)

Meaning: at home in many places or situation; internationally sophisticated

Use: Huey's interests were cosmopolitan. He liked Greek wine, German beer, Dutch cheese, Japanese cars and French fries.

Countenance (Noun)

Meaning: face, facial expression, especially an encouraging one

Use: His father's confident continence gave him the courage to persevere.

Covenant (Noun)

Meaning: a solemn agreement; a contract; a pledge each other anyone

Use: We signed a covenant in which we promised never to drive Harish's father's car without his permission.

Covert (Adjective)

Meaning: secret; hidden

Use: Covert activities are secret activities.

Covet (Verb)

Meaning: to wish for enviously

Use: Bitto coveted Bobby's bicycle and very nearly decided to steal it.

Credulous (Adjective)

Meaning: eager to believe, gullible

Use: Pooja was so credulous that she simply nodded happily when Raja told her he could teach her how to fly.

Criterion (Noun)

Meaning: standard; basis for judgement

Use: In choosing among the linemen, the most important criterion was quickness.

Cryptic (Adjective)

Meaning: mysterious; mystifying

Use: Asha's remarks were cryptic. Everyone was baffled by what she said.

Culinary (Adjective)

Meaning: relating to cooking or the kitchen

Use: A cooking school is sometimes called a culinary institute.

Culminate (Verb)

Meaning: to climax; to reach full effect

Use: The masked ball was the culmination of our fund-raising efforts.

Culpable (Adjective)

Meaning: deserving blame; guilty

Use: A person who is culpable is one who can be blamed for doing something.

Curtail (Verb)

Meaning: to shorten; to cut short

Use: The student curtailed his effort to cut the cat's tail with the lawn mower.

D

Dabber (Noun)

Meaning: stick for Colouring

Use: A dabber is used by printers to apply ink.

Daft (Adjective)

Meaning: silly, crazy

Use: He is a daft person.

Dale (Noun)

Meaning: long valley

Use: My farmhouses are all across the dale.

Damage (Noun)

Meaning: inquiry loss

Use: The Bomb damaged several buildings.

Dandle (Verb)

Meaning: to toss baby in arms or knee

Use: Somebody who was dandled on Queen's knee must appear an old fogy.

Daring (Noun)

Meaning: boldness

Use: She is a daring girl.

Dazzle (Verb)

Meaning: to overpower sight

Use: I was dazzled by the car's headlights.

Daunt (Verb)

Meaning: to make fearful; to intimidate

Use: The size of the players on the visiting team was daunting. The players on the home team began to perspire nervously.

Dearth (Noun)

Meaning: lack, scarcity

Use: There is no dearth of comedy at a convention of clowns.

Deal (Noun)

Meaning: to distribute

Use: The committee will deal with this complaint.

Debacle (Noun)

Meaning: violent breakdown; sudden overthrow

Use: A football game can turn into a debacle if one team is suddenly being clobbered.

Debilitate (Verb)

Meaning: to weaken; to cripple

Use: The football player's career was ended by a debilitating injury to his knee.

Decadent (Adjective)

Meaning: decaying or decayed, especially in terms of morals

Use: Spending the time in local bars instead of going to class is decadent.

Decimate (Verb)

Meaning: to kill or destroy a large part of

Use: To decimate an army is to come close to wiping it out.

Decorous (Adjective)

Meaning: proper; in good taste; orderly

Use: The New Year's Eve crowd was relatively decorous until midnight, when they went wild.

Decide (Verb)

Meaning: to resolve

Use: I have decided to retire, what decided you against

Deduce (Verb)

Meaning: to conclude from the evidence; to infer

Use: To deduce something is to conclude it without being told it directly.

Defame (Verb)

Meaning: to libel or slander; to ruin the good name of

Use: The local businessman accused the newspaper of defaming him by publishing an article that said his company was poorly managed.

Deference (Noun)

Meaning: submission to another's will, respect; courtesy

Use: The young man showed deference to his grandfather. He let the old man have first dibs on the birthday cake.

Definitive (Adjective)

Meaning: conclusive; providing the last word

Use: The army completely wiped out the invaders. Its victory was definitive.

Degenerate (Verb)

Meaning: break-down; to deteriorate

Use: The mood of the party was spoiled when a drunken degenerate wandered in from off the street.

Deleterious (Adjective)

Meaning: harmful

Use: Smoking cigarettes is deleterious to your health. So is brushing your teeth with oven cleaner or washing your hair with gasoline.

Delineate (Verb)

Meaning: describe accurately; to draw in outline

Use: Sharon's peculiar feelings about her pet gorilla were delineated in the newspaper article about her.

Delude (Verb)

Meaning: to deceive

Use: The deluded mental patient believed that he was a chicken sandwich.

Demagogue (Noun)

Meaning: a leader of the people, but more a rabble rouser

Use: Ajay is a demagogue of his group.

Depravity (Noun)

Meaning: extreme wickedness or corruption

Use: Mrs. Sethi wondered whether the depravity of her class of eight-year-olds was the result of their watching Saturday morning television.

Denizen (Noun)

Meaning: inhabitant

Use: Fish are sometimes referred to as denizens of the deep. Don't refer to them this way yourself. The expression is a cliché.

Deprecate (Verb)

Meaning: to express disapproval of

Use: To deprecate a colleague's work is to risk making yourself unwelcome in your colleague's office.

Deride (Verb)

Meaning: to ridicule; to laugh at contemptuously

Use: Sportswriters derided India's football team which hadn't won a game in many years.

Derogatory (Adjective)

Meaning: disapproving; degrading

Use: Om could never seem to think of anything nice to say about anyone. Virtually all his comments were derogatory.

Desiccate (Verb)

Meaning: to dry out

Use: Plums become prunes through a process of desiccation.

Despondent (Adjective)

Meaning: extremely depressed; full of despair

Use: The cook became despondent when the wedding cake exploded fifteen minutes before the reception.

Despot (Noun)

Meaning: an absolute ruler; an autocrat

Use: The manager of the office was a despot. Workers who disagreed with him were fired.

Destitute (Adjective)

Meaning: extremely poor; utterly lacking

Use: Destitute people are people without money or possessions or with very little money and very few possessions.

Desultory (Adjective)

Meaning: without a plan or purpose; disconnected; random

Use: Pushpa made a few desultory attempts to start a garden, but nothing came of them.

Dialectical (Adjective)

Meaning: relating to discussions; relating to the rules and methods of reasoning; approaching truth in the middle of opposing extremes

Use: The game of Twenty Questions is dialectical in that the participants attempt to narrow down a chosen object by asking a series of even more specific questions.

Dictum (Noun)

Meaning: an authoritative saying; an adage; a maxim; a proverb

Use: No pain no gain is a hackneyed dictum of sadistic coaches everywhere.

Diffident (Adjective)

Meaning: timid; lacking in self-confidence

Use: The diffident student never made a single comment in class.

Didactic (Adjective)

Meaning: intended to teach; morally instructive; pedantic

Use: The Priest's conversation was always didactic. He never said anything that wasn't intended to teach a lesson.

Digress (Adverb)

Meaning: to stray from the main subject

Use: After a lengthy digression, the lecturer returned to his speech and brought it to a conclusion.

Dilettante (Noun)

Meaning: someone with superficial knowledge of the arts; an amateur; a dabbler

Use: Helen dismissed the members of the sculpture club as nothing more than a bunch of dilettantes.

Discern (Verb)

Meaning: to have insight; to see things clearly, to discriminate; to differentiate

Use: The ill-mannered People at Rohit's party proved that he had little discernment when it came to choosing friends.

Discreet (Adjective)

Meaning: Prudent; judiciously reserved

Use: Raghu was very discreet; he only said what was necessary.

Discrete (Adjective)

Meaning: unconnected; separate; distinct

Use: The drop in the stock market was not the result of any single force but of many discrete trends.

Disdain (Noun)

Meaning: arrogant scorn; contempt

Use: Jimmy viewed the hot dog with disdain, believing that to eat such a disgusting food was beneath him.

Disinterested (Adjective)

Meaning: not taking sides; unbiased

Use: A disinterested observer is one who has no personal stake in or attachment to what is being observed.

Disparage (Verb)

Meaning: to belittle; to say uncomplimentary things about, usually in a somewhat indirect way

Use: The mayor disparaged our efforts to beautify the town square by saying that the flower bed we had planted looked somewhat worse than the weeds it had replaced.

Disparate (Adjective)

Meaning: different; incompatible; unequal

Use: Our interests were disparate. Sneha liked to play with dolls and I liked to throw her dolls out the window.

Disseminate (Verb)

Meaning: to spread the seeds of something, to scatter, to make widely known

Use: News is disseminated through many media; radio, television, newspapers, magazines, and gossips.

Dissipate (Verb)

Meaning: to thin out, drift away, or dissolve; to waste or squander

Use: The smoke dissipated as soon as we opened the windows.

Dissolution (Noun)

Meaning: the breaking up or dissolving of something into parts; disintegration

Use: Nothing could prevent the dissolution of the P. W. Herman Fan club after he retired to seek a political career.

Distend (Verb)

Meaning: to swell; to extend a great deal

Use: A distended belly is one symptom of malnutrition.

Distinguish (Verb)

Meaning: to tell apart; to cause to stand out

Use: His face had no distinguishing characteristics. There was nothing about his features that stuck in your memory.

Docile (Adjective)

Meaning: easily taught, obedient, easy to handle

Use: The baby raccoons appeared docile at first. But they were almost impossible to control.

Dock (Noun)

Meaning: basin in port for ships

Use: The ship was in dock for three weeks.

Doctrinaire (Adjective)

Meaning: inflexibly committed to a doctrine or theory without regard to its practicality

Use: A doctrinaire opponent of fluoridation of water would be someone whose opposition could not be shaken by proof that fluoride is good for teeth and not bad for anything else.

Dogmatic (Adjective)

Meaning: arrogantly assertive of unproven ideas, stubbornly claiming that something (often a system of beliefs) is beyond dispute

Use: Mahesh is dogmatic on the subject of the creation of the world. He sneers at anyone whose views are not identical to his.

Domestic (Adjective)

Meaning: having to do with the household or family; not foreign

Use: A home that enjoys domestic tranquility is a happy home.

Dominate (Adjective)

Meaning: to lord over

Use: Successful leaders dominate events rather than react to them.

Dormant (Adjective)

Meaning: inactive; as though asleep; asleep

Use: The volcano erupted violently and then fell dormant for several hundred years.

Doubt (Verb)

Meaning: too distrust

Use: He is doubtful about the future of the school.

Downcast (Adjective)

Meaning: with eyes looking down

Use: "He gave the girl a downcast glare." I hope that helps.

Drape (Verb)

Meaning: to hang

Use: Hang the drape over the window.

Draught (Noun)

Meaning: current of air

Use: We increase the heat in the furnace by increasing the draught.

Dray (Noun)

Meaning: low strong Cart

Use: We can see the large drays rolling up towards our camp.

Drench (Verb)

Meaning: to wet

Use: The war drenched the country in blood.

Drift (Noun)

Meaning: current, tendency

Use: Sanchita smiled from pure happiness, for she began to see the drift of things now.

Dual (Adjective)

Meaning: consisting of two

Use: The man used a dual blade for shaving.

Dubious (Adjective)

Meaning: full of doubt; uncertain

Use: I was fairly certain that I would be able to fly if I could merely flap my arms hard enough. But Manisha was dubious. She said I'd better flap my legs as well.

Duel (Noun)

Meaning: fight between two persons

Use: I have a duel match against your brother.

Duplicity (Noun)

Meaning: the act of being two-faced; double-dealing; deception

Use: Liars engage in duplicity all the time; they say one thing and do another.

Durability (Noun)

Meaning: durableness

Use: They advertised the durability of their products.

Duteous (Adjective)

Meaning: dutiful

Use: My son is a duteous son.

Dwarf (Noun)

Meaning: very small human being

Use: Shetland ponies are the dwarfs of the horse world.

Dye (Verb)

Meaning: to give colour to

Use: Raveena dyed the t-shirt in hues of red and blue.

Dyspepsia (Noun)

Meaning: indigestion

Use: Shruti is suffering from dyspepsia.

E

Eager (Adjective)

Meaning: ardent, earnest

Use: He is eager to travel abroad.

Eagre (Noun)

Meaning: large tidal wave

Use: Last night, I saw the eagers in sea.

Earn (Verb)

Meaning: to gain by labour, to deserve

Use: She earns a lot in her new job.

Eavesdrop (Verb)

Meaning: to listen secretly

Use: The jealous man was eavesdropping on his wife's conversation.

Ebullient (Adjective)

Meaning: boiling; bubbling with excitement; exuberant

Use: Monika was ebullient when her fairy godmother said she could use one of her three wishes to wish for three more wishes.

Eccentric (Adjective)

Meaning: not conventional; a little kooky; irregular

Use: The rocket followed an eccentric course; first it veered in one direction, then it veered in another, then it crashed.

Eclectic (Adjective)

Meaning: choosing the best from many sources; drawn from many sources

Use: George's eclectic reading made him well rounded.

Ecclesiastic (Adjective)

Meaning: priest, pertaining to church

Use: The ecclesiastical courts lost all jurisdictions over criminal acts in 1576.

Economic (Adjective)

Meaning: spendthrift

Use: The CEO is running this company with complete lack of understanding of basic economics.

Ecstasy (Noun)

Meaning: excessive joy

Use: He has been given a five year jail sentence for attempting to smuggle ecstasy into Israel from Netherlands.

Ecstatic (Adjective)

Meaning: rapturous, very delightful

Use: The hippie danced ecstatically.

Edge (Noun)

Meaning: sharp side of cutting instrument

Use: That gentleman sat on the edge of my bed.

Edible (Adjective)

Meaning: eatable

Meaning: Mom's cake wasn't great, but it was edible.

Edify (Verb)

Meaning: to enlighten; to instruct, especially in moral or religious matters

Use: The teacher's goal was to edify her students, not to force a handful of facts down their throats.

Efface (Verb)

Meaning: to erase; to rub away the features of

Use: We tried to efface the dirty words that had been written on the front of our house, but nothing would remove them.

Effect (Verb)

Meaning: to bring to pass

Use: Exposure to the sun had the effect of toughening his skin.

Effervesce (Verb)

Meaning: to boil with hissing noise

Use: Effervesce slightly in dilute hydrochloric and thus indicating calcite element.

Efficient (Adjective)

Meaning: competent

Use: The car engine was cleaner and more efficient.

Effort (Noun)

Meaning: attempt

Use: Effort force is the force used to moving an object over a distance.

Effusion (Noun)

Meaning: a pouring forth

Use: When the child was rescued from the well there was an intense effusion of emotion from the crowd that had gathered around the hole.

Eglantine (Noun)

Meaning: sweet brier

Use: The princess was crowned with eglantine.

Egocentric (Adjective)

Meaning: selfish; believing that one is the centre of everything

Use: Jatin was so egocentric that he could never give anyone else credit for doing anything.

Egregious (Adjective)

Meaning: extremely bad; flagrant

Use: The mother's egregious neglect was responsible for her child's accidental cross-country ride on the freight train.

Ejaculate (Verb)

Meaning: to utter words suddenly

Use: The mayor uttered a forceful ejaculation at the size of the crowd waiting to hear him speak.

Eject (Verb)

Meaning: to drive

Use: My mother told me to eject the DVD, so she could put it away in the case.

Ejection (Noun)

Meaning: expulsion

Use: The ejection of troublemakers by the police.

Elaborate (Verb)

Meaning: to produce with much labour

Use: Elaborate your work it could get better.

Elation (Noun)

Meaning: pride

Use: There was a lot of elation for parent's on graduation day.

Elder (Adjective)

Meaning: older

Use: There was something lordly in my elder brother and his fellows were ever subject to his will.

Electrode (Noun)

Meaning: an electrode is an electrical conductor used to make contact with a nonmetallic part of a circuit

Use: An electrodes are good conductor of electricity.

Electrolysis (Noun)

Meaning: process of chemical decomposition by electricity

Use: Electrodes are the main component use for electrolysis.

Element (Noun)

Meaning: substance which cannot be decomposed into anything

Use: The dog is needed track of element.

Elicit (Verb)

Meaning: to bring out; to call forth

Use: The defendant tried to elicit the sympathy of the jury by appearing at the trial in a wheelchair, but the jury convicted him anyway.

Elliptical (Adjective)

Meaning: oval; missing a word or words; obscure

Use: The orbit of the earth is not perfectly round, it is elliptical.

Elucidation (Verb)

Meaning: explanation

Use: You should serve for further elucidation of the subject.

Elusive (Adjective)

Meaning: hard to pin down; evasive

Use: The elusive criminal was next to impossible for the police to catch.

Emigrate (Verb)

Meaning: to move to a new country; to move to a new place to live; to expatriate

Use: The Soviet dissidents were persecuted by the secret police, so they sought permission to emigrate.

Eminent (Adjective)

Meaning: well known and respected; standing out from all others in quality or accomplishment; outstanding

Use: The entire audience fell silent when the eminent musician walked onto the stage and picked up his banjo and bongo drums.

Empirical (Adjective)

Meaning: relying on experience or observation; not merely theoretical

Use: The apple-dropping experiment gave the scientists empirical evidence that gravity exists.

Emulate (Verb)

Meaning: to strive to equal or excel, usually through imitation

Use: To emulate someone is to try to be just as good as, or better than, him or her.

Encroach (Verb)

Meaning: to make gradual or stealthy inroads into; to trespass.

Use: As the city grew, it encroached on the countryside surrounding it.

Endemic (Adjective)

Meaning: native; restricted to a particular region or era; indigenous

Use: That peculiar strain of influenza was endemic in a small community in East Delhi; there were no cases anywhere else.

Enervate (Verb)

Meaning: to reduce the strength or energy of, especially to do so gradually

Use: Mayank felt enervated by his long ordeal and couldn't make himself get out of bed.

Enfranchise (Verb)

Meaning: to grant the privileges of citizenship, especially the right to vote

Use: In India, citizens become enfranchised on their eighteenth birthdays.

Engender (Verb)

Meaning: to bring into existence; to create; to cause

Use: My winning lottery ticket engendered a great deal of envy among my co-workers. They all wished that they had won.

Enigma (Noun)

Meaning: a mystery

Use: Hal is an enigma. He never does any homework but he always gets good grades.

Enormity (Adjective)

Meaning: extreme evil, a hideous offense; immensity

Use: Hitler's soldiers stormed through the village, committing one enormity after another.

Ephemeral (Adjective)

Meaning: lasting a very short time

Use: Youth and flowers are all ephemeral. They're gone before you know it. Some friendships are ephemeral.

Epitome (Noun)

Meaning: a brief summary that captures the meaning of the whole; the perfect example of something; a paradigm

Use: Lokesh's freshman year was an epitome of the college experience. He made friends, missed classes, fell in love, and flunked out.

Equal (Adjective)

Meaning: of same size

Use: The manager decides to equalize the duties among all the employees in his office.

Equipment (Noun)

Meaning: outfit, requisites

Use: This factory floor is a showcase for automation and robotic equipment.

Equivocate (Verb)

Meaning: to use ambiguous expressions

Use: I suggested him to use equivocate language.

Equanimity (Noun)

Meaning: composure; calm

Use: The mother of four boys viewed the mud ball fight with equanimity; at least they weren't shooting bullets at one another.

Equitable (Adjective)

Meaning: fair

Use: King Solomon's decision was certainly equitable; each mother would receive half the child.

Eradicate (Verb)

Meaning: to uproot

Use: Their goal was to eradicate poverty.

Erupt (Verb)

Meaning: to burst forth

Use: My neighbour erupted in anger over the mess we had created near his garden.

Erudite (Adjective)

Meaning: scholarly; deeply learned

Use: The professor said things so erudite that none of us had the slightest idea of what he was saying.

Espouse (Verb)

Meaning: to support; to advocate

Use: Bert espoused so many causes that he sometimes had trouble remembering which side he was on.

Euphemism (Noun)

Meaning: a pleasant or inoffensive expression used in place of an unpleasant or offensive one

Use: Aunt Rosy, who couldn't bring herself to say the word death, said that Uncle George had taken the big bus uptown. Taking the big bus uptown was her euphemism for dying.

Evaporate (Verb)

Meaning: to pass off into vapour

Use: The small pool of water evaporated in the sunshine.

Evanescent (Adjective)

Meaning: fleeting, vanishing, happening for only the briefest period

Use: Meteors are evanescent. They last so briefly that it is hard to tell whether one has actually appeared.

Eviction (Noun)

Meaning: dispossession from lands

Use: Mr. Dass evicted from his land by his brother.

Evolution (Noun)

Meaning: gradual unfolding or development

Use: A crucial period in the evolution of modern physics.

Ewe (Noun)

Meaning: female sheep

Use: The ewe had two lambs.

Ewer (Noun)

Meaning: large jug

Use: In royal hotel, they serve water with ancient ewer.

Exacerbate (Verb)

Meaning: to make worse

Use: The window's grief was exacerbated by the minister's momentary inability to remember her dead husband's name.

Exacting (Adjective)

Meaning: extremely demanding, difficult, requiring great skill or care

Use: The surgeon's exacting task was to reconnect the patient's severed eye-lashes.

Exalt (Verb)

Meaning: to raise high, to glorify

Use: The manager decided to exalt the lowly batboy by asking him to pitch in the opening game of the World Series.

Exasperate (Verb)

Meaning: to annoy thoroughly, to make very angry, to try the patience of

Use: The child's insistence on hopping backward on one foot exasperated his mother, who was in a hurry.

Exemplify (Verb)

Meaning: to illustrate by example, to serve as a good example

Use: Varun participated in every class discussion and typed all of these papers. His teacher thought Varun exemplified the model student.

Exhaustive (Adjective)

Meaning: thorough, rigorous, complete, painstaking

Use: Before you use a parachute, you should examine it exhaustively for defects. Once you jump, your decision is irrevocable.

Exhort (Verb)

Meaning: to urge strongly, to give a serious warning to

Use: The coach used his bullhorn to exhort us to try harder.

Exigency (Noun)

Meaning: an emergency, an urgency

Use: An academic exigency: You haven't opened a book all term and the final is tomorrow morning.

Exonerate (Verb)

Meaning: to free completely from blame, to exculpate

Use: Our dog was exonerated when we discovered that it was in fact the cat that had eaten all the chocolate chip cookies.

Expatriate (Verb)

Meaning: to throw (someone) out of his or her native land, to move away from one's native land, to emigrate

Use: Hugo was fed up with his native country and so expatriated to America.

Expedient (Adjective)

Meaning: providing an immediate advantage, serving one's immediate self-interest, practical

Use: The candidate's position in favour of higher pay for teachers was an expedient one adopted for the national teachers' convention and abandoned shortly afterward.

Expedite (Verb)

Meaning: to speed up or ease the progress of

Use: The lawyer expedited the progress of our case through the courts by bribing a few judges.

Explicit (Adjective)

Meaning: clearly and directly expressed

Use: The machine's instructions were explicit. They told us exactly what to do.

Extol (Verb)

Meaning: to praise highly, to laud

Use: The millionaire extolled the citizen who returned his gold watch, and then rewarded him with a heartfelt handshake.

Extraneous (Adjective)

Meaning: unnecessary, irrelevant, extra

Use: The book's feeble plot was buried in a lot of extraneous material about a talking dog.

Extrapolate (Verb)

Meaning: to project or deduce from some-thing known, to infer

Use - Jagat came up with a probable recipe by extrapolating from the taste of the cookies he had eaten at the store.

Extricate (Verb)

Meaning: to free from a difficulty

Use: Samir had no trouble driving his car into the ditch, but he needed a tow truck to extricate it.

Extrovert (Verb)

Meaning: an open, outgoing person, a person whose attention is focused on others rather than on himself or herself

Use: The little girl was quite an extrovert. She walked boldly into the roomful of strange adults and struck up a friendly conversation.

Eye (Noun)

Meaning: organ of sight

Use: He has a good eye for understated fashion.

Eyebrow (Noun)

Meaning: hairy arch over eye

Use: Her eyebrows complement her beauty.

Eyelash (Noun)

Meaning: hair on eyelids apple

Use: Always applies black colour on eyelashes while doing make up.

Eyelet (Noun)

Meaning: small hole

Use: I have golden ring for my eyelet.

Eyelid (Noun)

Meaning: cover of eye

Use: In this game his eyelids would stay open no longer.

Eyesore (Noun)

Meaning: something offensive to eye

Use: Don't allow kids to see eyesore cartoons.

Eye-witness (Noun)

Meaning: one who can testify from his own observation

Use: Sunita is a eye-witness of her mother's murder.

Eyrie (Noun)

Meaning: nest of bird of prey

Use: I saw small eggs on that eyrie.

F

Fable (Noun)

Meaning: fictitious tale

Use: At night, I will read fables.

Fabrication (Noun)

Meaning: a lie, something made up

Use: My story about being the Prince of Wales was a fabrication. I'm really the King of Denmark.

Facetious (Adjective)

Meaning: humorous, not serious, clumsily humorous

Use: Dinesh was sent to the principal's office for making a facetious remark about the intelligence of the Math teacher.

Facile (Adjective)

Meaning: fluent, skilful in a superficial way, easy

Use: Joe's poems were facile rather than truly accomplished. If you read them closely, you soon realised they were filled with clichés.

Farcical (Adjective)

Meaning: absurd, ludicrous

Use: The serious play quickly turned farcical when the leading man's belt broke and his pants fell to his ankles.

Fastidious (Adjective)

Meaning: meticulous, demanding, finicky almost before they hit the floor

Use: Rahul was so fastidious in his work habits that he needed neither a wastebasket nor an eraser.

Fatalist (Noun)

Meaning: someone who believes that future events are already determined and that humans are powerless to change them

Use: Fatalist is closely related to the word fate. A fatalist is someone who believes that fate determines everything.

Fatuous (Adjective)

Meaning: foolish silly, idiotic

Use: Aayushi is so pretty that her suitors are often driven to fatuous acts of devotion. They are infatuated with her.

Faulty (Adjective)

Meaning: guilty of fault

Use: The teacher ordered the faulty students to leave the class for the day.

Favourite (Adjective)

Meaning: one preferred before others

Use: Shahrukh Khan is my favourite actor.

Fear (Noun)

Meaning: to be afraid of

Use: Being alone is my greatest fear.

Feasible (Adjective)

Meaning: practicable

Use: I found a feasible solution to your problem.

Feast (Noun)

Meaning: banquet rich enjoyment

Use: The king invited them to feast in the palace.

Fecund (Adjective)

Meaning: fertile, productive

Use: The philosopher's imagination was so fecund that ideas hopped out of him like so many baby rabbits.

Fauna (Noun)

Meaning: animals

Use: We saw little evidence of fauna on our walk through the woods. We did, however, see plenty of flora, or plants.

Felicity (Noun)

Meaning: happiness, skilfulness, especially at expressing things, adeptness

Use: Shakespeare wrote with great felicity. His works are filled with felicitous expressions.

Fellow (Noun)

Meaning: companion

Use: He's a quite nice fellow but I don't like him.

Felony (Noun)

Meaning: crime

Use: He committed a felony.

Feminine (Adjective)

Meaning: pertaining to girl or woman

Use: She never used her femininity to win the argument.

Fend (Verb)

Meaning: to ward off

Use: He is old enough to fend for himself.

Fermentation (Noun)

Meaning: chemical change by fermenting

Use: Anaerobic conversion happens in fermentation process.

Ferocious (Adjective)

Meaning: violent

Use: Tiger is a ferocious animal.

Fervor (Noun)

Meaning: great warmth or earnestness, ardor, zeal

Use: Avid baseball fans frequently display their fervor for the game by throwing food at bad players.

Fertile (Adjective)

Meaning: able to produce

Use: He fertilized his fields with manure.

Fetter (Verb)

Meaning: to restrain, to hamper

Use: In his pursuit of the Nobel Prize for physics, Professor Jenkins was fettered by his near-total ignorance of the subject.

Fetish (Noun)

Meaning: inanimate objects worshipped by savages

Use: It is good to dress well, but there is no need to make a fetish of it.

Feudalism (Noun)

Meaning: system under which vassals held land on condition of military services

Use: In 15th Century feudalism came to Europe economic.

Few (Adjective)

Meaning: not many

Use: We have few book in this library about geology.

Fibre (Noun)

Meaning: thread like parts in animal or vegetable tissue

Use: The dress was made of strong fibre.

Fickle (Adjective)

Meaning: changeable, inconstant

Use: I think that they are fickle regarding the decision.

Fiction (Noun)

Meaning: invented story

Use: I prefer reading fiction to hearing about real events.

Fidelity (Noun)

Meaning: faithfulness, loyalty

Use: The crusader's life was marked by fidelity to the cause of justice.

Fidget (Verb)

Meaning: to be restless

Use: He fidgeted with his notes while lecturing.

Fiery (Adjective)

Meaning: hot as fire

Use: She has a fiery temper.

Figment (Noun)

Meaning: invention

Use: He is a figment of new imaginations.

Figurative (Adjective)

Meaning: based on figures of speech, expressing something in terms usually used for something else, metaphorical

Use: When the Mayor said that the housing market had sprouted wings, he was speaking figuratively. The housing market hadn't really sprouted wings. It had merely grown so rapidly that it had almost seemed to fly.

Filial (Adjective)

Meaning: relating to son or daughter

Use: The man was happy to be back with his filial relations after years of imprisonment.

Filter (Verb)

Meaning: to strain liquids

Use: A filter is used to make sure that the oil is clean and does not contain any dirt

Final (Adjective)

Meaning: decisive

Use: The judge's decision is final.

Finance (Noun)

Meaning: money, revenue

Use: The government is worried about the state of country's finances.

Find (Verb)

Meaning: to come across

Use: He was struggling to find the old book.

Finery (Noun)

Meaning: showy clothes and ornaments

Use: She has finery collection in her almirah.

Finesse (Noun)

Meaning: skilful maneuvering, subtlety, craftiness

Use: The doctor sewed up the wound with finesse, making stitches so small one could scarcely see them.

Finite (Adjective)

Meaning: having limit or boundary

Use: human knowledge is finite, divine knowledge infinite.

Fiord (Noun)

Meaning: long narrow inlet of sea

Use: In Norway, there are number of fiord in sea.

Firearm (Noun)

Meaning: weapon discharged by means of explosive

Use: They took the firearms to defeat the enemy army.

Fist (Noun)

Meaning: clenched hand

Use: He shook his fist at me in anger.

Flagrant (Adjective)

Meaning: glaringly bad, notorious, scandalous

Use: A flagrant theft is stealing a car, for example, from the lot behind the police station.

Flaunt (Verb)

Meaning: to show off; to display ostentatiously

Use: The brand-new millionaire annoyed all his friends by driving around his old neighbourhood to flaunt his new Rolls-Royce.

Flout (Verb)

Meaning: to disregard something out of disrespect

Use: A driver flouts the traffic laws by driving through red lights and knocking down pedestrians.

Foible (Noun)

Meaning: a minor character flaw

Use: Barbara's foibles included a tendency to prefer dogs to people.

Forbear (Verb)

Meaning: to refrain from, to abstain

Use: Gautam forbore to punch me in the nose, even though I had told him that I thought he was a sniveling idiot.

Foment (Verb)

Meaning: to stir up, to instigate

Use: The bad news from abroad fomented pessimism among professional investors.

Forgo (Verb)

Meaning: to do without, to forbear

Use: We had some of the chocolate cake, and some of the chocolate mousse, and some of the chocolate cream pie, but we were worried about our weight so we decided to forgo the chocolate-covered potato chips. That is, we forwent them.

Forsake (Verb)

Meaning: to abandon, to renounce and to relinquish

Use: All the guru's followers had forsaken him, so he became a real estate developer and turned his temple into an apartment building.

Fortuitous (Adjective)

Meaning: accidental, occurring by chance

Use: The program's outcome was not the result of any plan but was entirely fortuitous.

Foster (Verb)

Meaning: to nourish

Use: She fostered the child's talents.

Founder (Verb)

Meaning: to frail, to collapse, to sink

Use: The candidate's campaign for the presidency foundered when it was revealed that he had once been married to an orangutan.

Foundation (Noun)

Meaning: act of establishing

Use: Mr Mohan arranged funds to keep the foundation of this hospital.

Fraternal (Adjective)

Meaning: like brothers

Use: There was a lot of frenetic activity in the office, but nothing ever seemed to get accomplished.

Frugal (Adjective)

Meaning: economical, penny-pinching

Use: Lalita was so frugal that she even tried to bargain with the checkout girl at supermarket.

Fuel (Noun)

Meaning: material use for burning

Use: The machine ran out of fuel.

Fugacious (Adjective)

Meaning: fleeting

Use: Botany lasting for only a short time fugacious petals.

Fulgent (Adjective)

Meaning: shining

Use: Tower searchlights are as fulgent as half a billion candles.

Fumigate (Verb)

Meaning: to fume for destroying infection

Use: In hospital, fumigate is used to clear floors.

Function (Noun)

Meaning: duty or work

Use: Your function is to keep track on other workers.

Funeral (Adjective)

Meaning: pertaining to burial

Use: If he doesn't meet the deadline, it's his funeral.

Furbish (Verb)

Meaning: to clean

Use: He furbishes the wooden floor.

Furious (Adjective)

Meaning: very angry

Use: The furious pace of the trading floor.

Furtive (Adjective)

Meaning: secretive, sly

Use: John wiggled his ears while the countess was talking to him in a furtive attempt to catch our attention.

Further (Adverb)

Meaning: to greater distance or disagree

Use: There is no further news.

Fusee (Noun)

Meaning: conical pulley or wheel

Use: Fusee is used in wall clocks to maintain the mechanism.

Fusible (Adjective)

Meaning: fit to be melted or joined

Use: Rivers filled to overflowing by fusible snow.

Fusion (Noun)

Meaning: act of fusing

Use: The fusion of copper and zinc to form brass.

Fusty (Adjective)

Meaning: stale – smelling

Use: His house is fusty.

Futile (Adjective)

Meaning: useless, hopeless

Use: Our attempt to change the behaviour of Harvard was futile, but Lucinda hoped against hope.

Future (Adjective)

Meaning: about to happen

Use: He was afraid of what the future might bring.

Futurity (Noun)

Meaning: future time or life

Use: Everyone hopes for a better futurity.

Fuzz (Noun)

Meaning: fine particle or fibre

Use: The peaches were covered with fuzz.

Fuzzy (Adjective)

Meaning: full of fuz

Use: The television picture was fuzzy.

G

Gab (Noun)

Meaning: idle talk

Use: She was gabbing about her grandchildren.

Gabbler (Noun)

Meaning: chatterer

Use: Sita is a gabbler.

Gaffer (Noun)

Meaning: old rustic

Use: This television wires are gaffer.

Gain (Noun)

Meaning: profit, advance

Use: His views were once unacceptable but are now going ground rapidly.

Gaiter (Noun)

Meaning: covering for ankle

Use: I have gaiter for my feet.

Galaxy (Noun)

Meaning: luminous band of stars

Use: Our galaxy is known as Milky Way galaxy.

Gallant (Adjective)

Meaning: brave, noble

Use: He was a thoughtful, gallant and generous man.

Galley (Noun)

Meaning: low one decked ship

Use: He stood at the galley and waved his friends goodbye.

Galore (Noun)

Meaning: plenty, abundance

Use: There are book-shops galore in this town.

Gangster (Noun)

Meaning: member of gang of ruffians

Use: He was gangster in his time.

Gaol (Noun)

Meaning: prison, jail

Use: The murder was sent to gaol for rest of his life.

Garble (Verb)

Meaning: to select unfairly

Use: They garbled the CEO.

Gargle (Noun)

Meaning: liquid for washing throat

Use: Use ayurvedic medicines for Gargles.

Garnish (Verb)

Meaning: to decorate

Use: Parsley is often used to garnish salads.

Garth (Noun)

Meaning: garden, yard

Use: His house is surrounded by a beautiful Garth.

Gash (Noun)

Meaning: long and deep cut

Use: He has a gash on his cheek.

Gaunt (Adjective)

Meaning: thin

Use: She is a gaunt old woman.

Garrulous (Adjective)

Meaning: talkative, chatty

Use: Vinay is gregarious and garrulous. He loves to hang out with the gang and gab.

Genteel (Adjective)

Meaning: refined, polite, aristocratic, affecting refinement

Use: The ladies at the ball were too genteel to accept our invitation to the wrestling match.

Genre (Noun)

Meaning: a type or category, especially of art or writing

Use: The novel is one genre. Poetry is another. Alan displayed a great talent for a particular genre: the bawdy limerick.

Genuine (Adjective)

Meaning: real, pure

Use: He shows a genuine desire to improve.

Generosity (Noun)

Meaning: liberality

Use: A scholarship funded by the generosity of anonymous doors.

Genius (Noun)

Meaning: evil spirit

Use: The new professor of mathematics has been described as a genius.

Gentle (Adjective)

Meaning: noble, kind

Use: That doctor was very gentle.

Geographer (Noun)

Meaning: one who versed in geography

Use: Mohit is a geographer.

Geometry (Noun)

Meaning: science which treats measurement of lines and angles

Use: I like geometry rather than algebra.

Gesticulate (Verb)

Meaning: to make gestures, especially when speaking or in place of speaking

Use: Harit gesticulated wildly on the other side of the theater in an attempt to get out attention.

Gibbon (Noun)

Meaning: long armed ape

Use: Gibbons are found in Southeast Asia.

Gigantic (Adjective)

Meaning: huge giant like

Use: Last night, there were gigantic waves in the sea.

Giggle (Verb)

Meaning: to laugh like silly person

Use: She is a giggly young girl.

Gimlet (Noun)

Meaning: instrument for boring holes

Use: Carpenters used gimlet for screwing the woods.

Girder (Noun)

Meaning: supporting beam of wood or iron

Use: The girders of the bridge have collapsed.

Glace (Adjective)

Meaning: having smooth or polished surface

Use: In hilly areas, ice has glace.

Gladiator (Noun)

Meaning: fighter with sword

Use: One can find gladiator in stories of ancient Rome.

Glamorous (Noun)

Meaning: enchanting

Use: She wants to be a glamorous star.

Glazier (Noun)

Meaning: one who glazes windows

Use: Only the glazier can design this window beautifully.

Gleam (Noun)

Meaning: beam of light

Use: His red sports car gleamed in the sun.

Gloaming (Noun)

Meaning: dusk

Use: She likes to walk in gloaming dusky.

Glorify (Verb)

Meaning: to make glorious

Use: Your descriptions have glorified an average house into a mansion.

Glossy (Adjective)

Meaning: bright, shining

Use: I suggested her to use glossy paper for decoration.

Glozer (Noun)

Meaning: flatterer

Use: Be aware form Sanjay, he is a glozer.

Glut (Noun)

Meaning: surplus, an overabundance

Use: The international oil shortage turned into an international oil glut with surprising speed.

Glutton (Noun)

Meaning: one who eats to excess

Use: The child is fat because he is such a glutton.

Gnarl (Verb)

Meaning: to growl

Use: The wind has gnarled this old tree.

Gobble (Verb)

Meaning: to swallow hastily

Use: You will be sick if you keep gobbling your meals like that.

Goblin (Noun)

Meaning: spirit, demon

Use: Don't tell a frightening fairy-story about goblins.

Gong (Noun)

Meaning: heavy sonorous metal

Use: The dinner gong.

Goodwill (Noun)

Meaning: friendly

Use: I invited them to dinner as a gesture of goodwill.

Gorgeous (Adjective)

Meaning: splendid

Use: That red haired man in the gorgeous uniform of a Marshal of the empire.

Gory (Adjective)

Meaning: covered with blood

Use: The film is full of gory death scenes.

Grandiloquent (Adjective)

Meaning: pompous, using a lot of big, fancy words in an attempt to sound impressive

Use: The new minister's grandiloquence got him in trouble with deacons who wanted him to be more restrained in his sermons.

Grandiose (Adjective)

Meaning: absurdly exaggerated

Use: The scientist's grandiose plan was to build a hug shopping centre on the surface of the moon.

Gratuitous (Adjective)

Meaning: given freely (said of something bad), unjustified, unprovoked, uncalled for

Use: Their attack against us was gratuitous. We had never done anything to offend them.

Gravity (Noun)

Meaning: seriousness

Use: The anchorman's nervous giggling was entirely inappropriate, given the gravity of the situation.

Gregarious (Adjective)

Meaning: sociable, enjoying the company of others

Use: Lalit was too gregarious to enjoy the fifty years he spent in solitary confinement.

Grenadier (Noun)

Meaning: soldier who throws explosive shell by hand

Use: Captain Ritesh is a grenadier of our regiment.

Grievance (Noun)

Meaning: hardship, complaint

Use: They felt they had a legitimate grievance.

Gristle (Noun)

Meaning: flexible bones of young ones

Use: There's too much gristle in this steak.

Guardian (Noun)

Meaning: one having care of person

Use: He became the child's guardian when her parents died.

Guest (Noun)

Meaning: one entertained at another house

Use: we are having guests for dinner.

Guile (Noun)

Meaning: cunning, duplicity; artfulness

Use: Janak used guile, not intelligence, to win the spelling bee. He cheated.

Guilt (Noun)

Meaning: crime, sin

Use: Fingerprints proved the murder's guilt.

Gullet (Noun)

Meaning: throat, food pipe

Use: He burnt his mouth, throat and gullet.

Gum (Noun)

Meaning: adhesive substance got from some plants

Use: We can stick these pictures into the book with gum.

Gurgle (Verb)

Meaning: to make bubbling sound

Use: The baby gurgled with pleasure.

Gush (Verb)

Meaning: to rush forth

Use: The lady kept gushing about her husband's success.

Gust (Noun)

Meaning: sudden blast of wind

Use: Gusts of wind of up to eighty kilometres an hour.

Guttle (Verb)

Meaning: to eat like glutton

Use: He guttled three sandwiches.

Guzzle (Verb)

Meaning: to swallow greedily

Use: The boys guzzled the cheap vodka.

Gymnast (Noun)

Meaning: expert in gymnastics

Use: Rakesh is a best gymnast from Nagpur.

Gynaecology (Noun)

Meaning: science dealing with women's disease

Use: She has chosen gynaecology as a stream in her medical life.

Gyrate (Verb)

Meaning: to whirl round

Use: Stock prices gyrated around last week's high.

Gyrograph (Noun)

Meaning: instrument recording revolutions

Use: Green revolution can be seen through gyrograph.

H

Habiliment (Noun)

Meaning: garment

Use: He is surrounded by the habiliments of the television news industry.

Habitual (Adjective)

Meaning: acquired by habit

Use: He soon recovered his habitual geniality.

Hackneyed (Adjective)

Meaning: overused, trite, stale

Use: Manik's book was full of clichés and hackneyed phrases.

Haggish (Adjective)

Meaning: ugly

Use: Her grandmother is a haggish lady.

Hallucinate (Verb)

Meaning: to produce false impression on mind

Use: Rehana stared at him, as if were hallucinating.

Halyard (Noun)

Meaning: rope for raising or lowering sails

Use: He tried to slow the boat with halyard.

Hamper (Verb)

Meaning: to obstruct

Use: I tried to run away but I was hampered by my long dress.

Handicraft (Noun)

Meaning: manual occupation

Use: My new handicraft was seashell pictures.

Handloom (Noun)

Meaning: loom worked by hand

Use: I love to do handloom work.

Harbinger (Noun)

Meaning: a forerunner, a signal of

Use: Warm weather is the harbinger of spring.

Hapless (Adjective)

Meaning: unlucky

Use: Joe's hapless search for fun led him from one disappointment to another.

Harass (Verb)

Meaning: to distress

Use: The army was constantly harassed by groups of terrorists.

Hasty (Adjective)

Meaning: speedy

Use: After the hasty meal, army took up their positions.

Haughtiness (Noun)

Meaning: pride

Use: She lacks the arrogance and haughtiness of so many musical arts.

Haul (Verb)

Meaning: to drag

Use: Horses are used to haul barges along canals.

Hazard (Noun)

Meaning: risk, danger

Use: Space travel is full of hazards.

Headquarters (Noun)

Meaning: chief centre

Use: The company has its headquarters in Mumbai.

Health (Noun)

Meaning: sound state of body

Use: I may be getting old, but so long as I keep my health.

Heaven (Noun)

Meaning: abode of God and his angles

Use: This is heaven; she said, lying on the beach in the sun.

Hedge (Noun)

Meaning: fence of bushes or shrubs

Use: He was hedged in by his own shyness.

Hedonism (Noun)

Meaning: the pursuit of pleasure as a way of life

Use: A hedonist practices hedonism twenty-four hours a day.

Hegemony (Noun)

Meaning: leadership, especially of one nation over another

Use: America's nuclear hegemony has been challenged and perhaps usurped by the Soviets.

Helve (Noun)

Meaning: handle of weapon

Use: He grabbed the hammer by the helve.

Hemp (Noun)

Meaning: fibrous or intoxicant

Use: Dried leaves of hemp plant used in medicines.

Heptarchy (Noun)

Meaning: government

Use: The seven principal concurrent early English heptarchy.

Herculean (Adjective)

Meaning: very strong, very difficult

Use: His shoulders were Herculean with long arms.

Heresy (Noun)

Meaning: any belief that is strongly opposed to established beliefs

Use: Galileo was tried for the heresy of suggesting that the sun did not revolve around the earth. He was almost convicted of being a heretic, but he recanted his heretical view.

Hermetic (Adjective)

Meaning: impervious to external influence, airtight

Use: The president led a hermetic existence in the White House, as his advisers attempted to seal him off from the outside world.

Hesitate (Verb)

Meaning: to be in doubt

Use: I hesitate to say he lied but he certainly misled me.

Hesperian (Adjective)

Meaning: western

Use: She likes Hesperian culture.

Heterogeneous (Adjective)

Meaning: of different kinds

Use: The population of India is vast and heterogeneous.

Heyday (Noun)

Meaning: golden age, prime

Use: In his heyday, Vernon was a world-class athlete. Today he's just Vernon.

Hiatus (Noun)

Meaning: a break or interruption, often from work

Use: Sachin looked forward to spring break as a welcome hiatus from the rigors of campus parties.

Hideous (Adjective)

Meaning: very ugly

Use: She saw a hideous face at the window and screamed.

Hierarchy (Noun)

Meaning: an organisation based on rank or degree, pecking order

Use: Even in the desert there was a kind of social hierarchy.

Hieroglyph (Noun)

Meaning: picture-writing

Use: In early ages people use hieroglyph for communication.

Hilarious (Adjective)

Meaning: merry joyous

Use: He has a collection of hilarious tales.

Hindrance (Noun)

Meaning: obstruction

Use: Higher rates have been a hindrance to economic recovery.

Histrionic (Adjective)

Meaning: overly dramatic, theatrical

Use: The chairman's histrionic Presentation convinced no one.

Hobble (Verb)

Meaning: to limp along

Use: The old lady hobbled along with a stick.

Hocuse (Verb)

Meaning: to cheat

Use: Don't do things to hocuse her.

Hodge (Noun)

Meaning: rustic

Use: Rakesh is a typical name for a rust labour.

Hoist (Verb)

Meaning: to raise aloof

Use: He hoisted the child up on to his shoulders.

Hollow (Adjective)

Meaning: excavated, empty

Use: The local team was beaten hollow by eight goals to one on Saturday.

Holster (Noun)

Meaning: leather case for pistol

Use: He always keeps his pistol in holster.

Homily (Noun)

Use: a sermon

Meaning: The football coach often began practice with a lengthy homily on the virtues of clean living.

Homogeneous (Adjective)

Meaning: uniform, made entirely of one thing

Use: The kindergarten class was extremely homogeneous: all the children had blond hair, blue eyes, red shoes, and the same last name.

Honorarium (Noun)

Meaning: fee paid for professional services

Use: What is your honorarium for this work.

Honorary (Adjective)

Meaning: serving without pay

Use She is the council's honorary secretary.

Horizon (Noun)

Meaning: line where

Use: The sun had already sunk below the horizon.

Horrible (Adjective)

Meaning: dreadful

Use: I have made some horrible mistakes.

Horticultural (Noun)

Meaning: art of growing flowers, fruits and vegetables

Use: She grew very beautiful flowers in her horticultural classes.

Hostage (Noun)

Meaning: person kept in another's custody as pledge

Use: The police were unable to attack the terrorist because they were holding three people hostage.

Hostile (Adjective)

Meaning: showing enmity

Use: The two countries were engaged in hostilities.

Hour (Noun)

Meaning: sixty minutes

Use: He spent an hour trying to start the car this morning.

Hover (Verb)

Meaning: to remain in air aloft

Use: She hovered between leaving and staying.

Hoyden (Noun)

Meaning: romping girl

Use: She is like a hoyden.

Humanity (Noun)

Meaning: human race or nature

Use: They face charges of committing crimes against humanity.

Humidity (Noun)

Meaning: moisture

Use: The heat and humidity were insufferable.

Humorous (Adjective)

Meaning: amusing

Use: It was a humorous story.

Husbandry (Noun)

Meaning: management of resources, livestock farming

Use: Everyone husbanded oil and electricity during the energy crisis of the seventies.

Hurricane (Noun)

Meaning: violent storm

Use: People have been killed in the hurricane's destructive path.

Hydrant (Noun)

Meaning: pipe in streets for drawing water from water main

Use: In city, the people are using hydrant to store water.

Hydrophobia (Noun)

Meaning: disease, caused by bite of mad dog

Use: He died because of hydrophobia.

Hyperbole (Noun)

Meaning: an exaggeration used as a figure of speech, exaggeration

Use: When Jatin said, I'm so hungry I could eat a horse, he was using a hyperbole to convey the extent of his hunger.

Hypothetical (Adjective)

Meaning: uncertain, unproven

Use: Raj's skill as a baseball player was entirely hypothetical, since he had never played the game.

Hygiene (Noun)

Meaning: science of health

Use: Hygienic conditions are essential in hospital.

I

Iconoclast (Noun)

Meaning: one who attacks popular beliefs or institutions

Use: The popular columnist was an inveterate iconoclast, avidly attacking public figures no matter what their party affiliation.

Ideology (Noun)

Meaning:. a system of social or political ideas

Use: Conservatism and liberalism are competing ideologies.

Idiosyncrasy (Noun)

Meaning: a peculiarity, an eccentricity

Use: The doctor's interest was aroused by an idiosyncrasy in Bill's skull: there seemed to be a coin slot in the back of his head.

Idyllic (Adjective)

Meaning: charming in a rustic way, naturally peaceful

Use: They built their house in an idyllic spot. There was a babbling brook in back and an unbroken view of wooded hills in front.

Ignominy (Noun)

Meaning: deep disgrace

Use: After the big scandal, the formerly high-flying investment banker fell into a life of shame and ignominy.

Illicit (Adjective)

Meaning: illegal, not permitted

Use: Criminals engage in illicit activities.

Imminent (Adjective)

Meaning: just about to happen

Use: The pink glow in the east made it clear that sunrise was imminent.

Impartial (Adjective)

Meaning: fair, not favouring one side or the other, unbiased

Use: Jurors are supposed to be impartial rather than partial. They aren't supposed to make up their minds until they've heard all the evidence.

Immutable (Adjective)

Meaning: unchangeable

Use: Jimmy's mother had only one immutable rule: no dancing on the dinner table.

Impeccable (Adjective)

Meaning: flawless, entirely without sin

Use: Hal's clothes were always impeccable. Even the wrinkles were perfectly creased.

Imperial (Adjective)

Meaning: like an emperor or an empire

Use: Imperial, emperor and empire are all derived from the same root.

Impervious (Adjective)

Meaning: not allowing anything to pass through, impenetrable

Use: A raincoat, if it is any good, impervious to water. It is made of an impervious material.

Impetuous (Adjective)

Meaning: impulsive, extremely impatient

Use: Samantha was so impetuous that she never took more than a few seconds to make up her mind.

Impotent (Adjective)

Meaning: powerless, helpless, unable to perform sexual intercourse

Use: Joe and Betty made a few impotent efforts to turn aside the steamroller, but it squished their vegetable garden anyway.

Implement (Verb)

Meaning: to carry out

Use: The government was better at creating new laws than at implementing them.

Impugn (Verb)

Meaning: to attack, especially to attack the truth or integrity of something

Use: The critic impugned the originally of Jacob's novel, claiming that long stretches of it had been lifted from the work of someone else.

Inane (Adjective)

Meaning: silly, senseless

Use: Their plan to make an indoor swimming pool by flooding their basement was inane.

Inaugurate (Verb)

Meaning: to begin officially, to induct formally into office

Use: The mayor inaugurated the new no-smoking policy and then celebrated by lighting up a big cigar.

Incandescent (Adjective)

Meaning: brilliant, giving off heat or light off light when it is heated

Use: An incandescent person is one who gives off light or energy in a figurative sense.

Incantation (Noun)

Meaning: a chant, the repetition of statements or phrases in a way reminiscent of a chant

Use: The students quickly became deaf to the principal's incantations about the importance of school spirit.

Incessant (Adjective)

Meaning: unceasing

Use: I will go deaf and lose my mind if you children don't stop your incessant bickering.

Incense (Verb)

Meaning: to make very angry

Use: My comment about his lovely painting of a tree incensed the artist, who said it was actually a portrait of his mother.

Incipient (Adjective)

Meaning: beginning, emerging

Use: Sitting in class, Henrietta detected an incipient tingle of boredom that told her she would soon be asleep.

Incisive (Adjective)

Meaning- cutting right to the heart of the matter

Use: After hours of debate, Louis offered a few incisive comments that made it immediately clear to everyone how dumb the original idea had been.

Incongruous (Adjective)

Meaning: not harmonious, not consistent, not appropriate, not fitting in

Use: The ultra-modern kitchen seemed incongruous in the restored eighteenth-century farmhouse. It was an incongruity.

Incorrigible (Adjective)

Meaning: incapable of being reformed

Use: The convict was an incorrigible criminal; as soon as he got out of prison.

Increment (Noun)

Meaning: an increase, one in a series of increases

Use: This year's fund-raising total represented an increment of 10 percent over last year's.

Indifferent (Adjective)

Meaning: not caring one way or the other, apathetic, mediocre

Use: Red was indifferent about politics. He didn't care who was elected to office so long as one passed a law against Monday Night Football.

Indigenous (Adjective)

Meaning: native, originating in that area

Use: Fast-food restaurants are indigenous to America, where they were invented.

Indigent (Adjective)

Meaning: poor

Use: The indigent family had little to eat, nothing to spend, and virtually nothing to wear.

Indolent (Adjective)

Meaning: lazy

Use: The indolent teenagers slept late, moped around and never looked for summer jobs.

Indignant (Adjective)

Meaning: angry, especially as a result of something unjust or unworthy, insulted

Use: Bruno became indignant when the policeman accused him of stealing the nuclear weapon.

Ineffable Adjective)

Meaning: incapable of being expressed or described

Use: The simple beauty of nature is often so ineffable that it brings tears to our eyes.

Indulgent (Adjective)

Meaning: allowing, conceding

Use: The nice mom was indulgent of her children, letting them have all the candy, cookies, and ice cream that they wanted, even for breakfast.

Inept (Adjective)

Meaning: clumsy, incompetent, gauche

Use: Joshua is an inept dancer. He is as likely to stomp on his partner's foot as he is to step on it.

Inert (Adjective)

Meaning: inactive, sluggish, not reaching chemically

Use: Having colds made the children inert and reluctant to get out of bed.

Inexorable (Adjective)

Meaning: relentless, inevitable, unavoidable

Use: Inexorable death finds everyone sooner or later.

Infamous (Adjective)

Meaning: shamefully wicked: having an extremely bad reputation, disgraceful

Use: Deep within the prison was the infamous torture chamber, where hooded guards tickled their prisoners with feathers until they confessed.

Infatuated (Adjective)

Meaning: foolish; foolishly passionate or attracted, made foolish, foolishly in love

Use: My ride in Boris's racing car infatuated me. I knew immediately that I would have to have a racing car too.

Infer (Verb)

Meaning: to conclude, to deduce

Use: She hadn't heard the score, but the silence in the locker room led her to infer that we had lost.

Infinitesimal (Adjective)

Meaning: very, very, very small, infinitely small

Use: Dummy old Willy's brain, if he had one at all, was undoubtedly infinitesimal.

Ingenuous (Adjective)

Meaning: frank, without deception, simple, artless, charmingly naïve

Use: A young child is ingenuous. He doesn't know much about the ways of the world, and certainly not enough to deceive anyone.

Inherent (Adjective)

Meaning: part of the essential nature of something, intrinsic

Use: There is an inherent strength in steel that is lacking from cardboard.

Injunction (Noun)

Meaning: a command or order, especially a court order

Use: Wendy's neighbours got a court injunction prohibiting her from playing her radio loud.

Innocuous (Adjective)

Meaning: harmless, banal

Use: The supposedly obscene record sounded pretty innocuous to us. There weren't even any four-letter words in it.

Innate (Adjective)

Meaning: existing since birth, inborn, inherent

Use: Vivek's kindness was innate. It was part of his natural character.

Inordinate (Adjective)

Meaning: excessive, unreasonable

Use: The young math teacher paid an inordinate amount of attention to the pretty blond senior.

Insatiable (Adjective)

Meaning: hard or impossible to satisfy, greedy, avaricious

Use: Rajesh has insatiable desire for luxurious things.

Insidious (Adjective)

Meaning: treacherous, sneaky

Use: Winter was insidious. It crept in under the doors and through cracks in the windows.

Insinuate (Verb)

Meaning: to hint, to creep in

Use: When I told her that I hadn't done any laundry in a month, Valerie insinuated that I was a snob.

Insipid (Adjective)

Meaning: dull, bland, banal

Use: We were bored to death at the party. It was full of insipid people making insipid conversation.

Insolent (Adjective)

Meaning: arrogant, insulting

Use- The ill-mannered four-year-old was so insolent that even adults were tempted to kick him in the rear end.

Instigate (Verb)

Meaning: to provoke, to stir up

Use: The strike was instigated by the ambitious union president who wanted to get his name into the newspapers.

Insular (Adjective)

Meaning: like an island, isolated

Use: Lying flat on his back in bed for twenty-seven years, the 1,200-pound man led an insular existence.

Insurgent (Noun)

Meaning: a rebel, someone who revolts against a government

Use: The heavily armed insurgents rushed into the presidential place, but they paused to taste the fresh blueberry pie on the dinner table and the president's bodyguards captured them.

Integral (Adjective)

Meaning: essential

Use: A solid offense was an integral part of our football team. So was a strong defence.

Intransigent (Adjective)

Meaning: uncompromising, stubborn

Use: Roy was an intransigent hard-liner and he didn't care how many people he offended with his views.

Intractable (Adjective)

Meaning: uncontrollable, stubborn, disobedient

Use: The intractable child was a torment to his nursery school teacher.

Intrinsic (Adjective)

Meaning: part of the essential nature of something, inherent

Use: Larry's intrinsic boldness was always getting him into trouble.

Introspective (Adjective)

Meaning: tending to think about oneself, examining one's feelings

Use: Rompy's introspective examination of his motives led him to conclude that he must have been at fault in the breakup of his marriage.

Inundate (Verb)

Meaning: to flood, to cover completely with water, to overwhelm

Use: The fifteen-year-old-girl was inundated with telegrams and gifts after she gave birth to octuplet.

Invective (Noun)

Meaning: insulting or abusive speech

Use: Herman wasn't much of an orator, but he was brilliant at invective.

Itinerant (Adjective)

Meaning: moving from place to place

Use: The life of a traveling salesman is an itinerant one.

Irascible (Adjective)

Meaning: easily angered or provoked, irritable

Use: A grouch is irascible. The students generally abused substitute teachers, but they knew that even substitute teachers become irascible on Monday mornings.

Ironic (Adjective)

Meaning: meaning the opposite of what you seem to say, using words to mean something other than what they seem to mean

Use: Ritesh was being ironic when he said he loved Pummy like a brother. In truth, he hated him.

Irrevocable (Adjective)

Meaning: irreversible

Use: Shortly after his car began to plunge toward the sea, Tom decided not to drive off the cliff after all, but by that point his decision to do so was irrevocable.

Inveterate (Adjective)

Meaning: habitual, firm in habit, deeply rooted

Use: Larry's practice of spitting into the fireplace became inveterate despite his wife's protestations.

J

Jabber (Verb)

Meaning: to talk idly, rapidly and indistinctly

Use: The women are always jabbering with one another.

Jacinth (Noun)

Meaning: precious stone of orange colour

Use: I have a necklace of Jacinth.

Jack-boots (Noun)

Meaning: boots reaching up to knees

Use: I like Jack-boots.

Jaconet (Noun)

Meaning: cotton cloth of medium thickness

Use: Jaconet is also used for bandages.

Jackal (Noun)

Meaning: a type of wild animal similar to a dog or wolf

Use: Jackal is the canine mammal of the genus Canis.

Jackpot (Noun)

Meaning: any outstanding award in any game like playing cards, poker etc.

Use: She must have hit the jackpot with the sales of her last album.

Jacuzzi (Noun)

Meaning: a system of underwater jets that keep the water in a bath or pool constantly agitated

Use: Jacuzzi is very expensive to use at home.

Jaguar (Noun)

Meaning: a large feline mammal of central and south America, closely related to the leopard and having a tawny coat spotted with black rosettes

Use: Some classifications consider Jaguar as a member of the genus Felis.

Jail (Noun)

Meaning: a place for the confinement of persons in lawful detentions, especially person awaiting trial under local Jurisdiction

Use: He jailed for two years.

Jamb (Noun)

Meaning: side post of door or fireplace

Use: Do not use Jamb for exit.

Janitor (Noun)

Meaning: care taker

Use: My mother was the janitor in the town school.

Jar (Verb)

Meaning: to make harsh sound, to dispute......

Use: She poured the jam into large jars.

Jasper (Noun)

Meaning: kind of quartz

Use: I want jasper in my ring.

Jaw (Noun)

Meaning: the two bones of the mouth in which the teeth are set

Use: The Crocodile's jaw opened wide.

Jaunty (Adjective)

Meaning: sprightly

Use: The novel is altogether jauntier than these quotations imply.

Jealous (Adjective)

Meaning: having feeling of dislike for any possible rivals

Use: She is jealous of her sister.

Jean (Noun)

Meaning: twilled cotton cloth

Use: I m more comfortable in jeans.

Jelly (Noun)

Meaning: juice of fruits boiled with sugar

Use: I have made raspberry jelly for the party.

Jennet (Noun)

Meaning: small Spanish horse

Use: You can find Jennet in Spain.

Jeopardous (Adjective)

Meaning: exposed to danger

Use: His office back door was jeopardous as its opening to electric room.

Jester (Noun)

Meaning: one who jests

Use: He is the class jester writ large.

Jest (Noun)

Meaning: a joke; something done or said to cause amusement

Use: In former times, a man employed in the courts of kings, nobles etc to amuse them with jest etc.

Jetty (Noun)

Meaning: landing pier

Use: Schooners are moored off wooden jetties.

Jewellery (Noun)

Meaning: jewels in general

Use: Rita is fond of jewellery.

Jiggle (Verb)

Meaning: jerk lightly

Use: The television picture kept jiggling up and down.

Jobbery (Noun)

Meaning: corrupt dealings

Use: He dealt with jobbery.

Jocular (Noun)

Meaning: one who characterized by joking and good humour

Use: Ravi is a Jocular.

Jocund (Adjective)

Meaning: joyful

Use: He is a Jocund person.

Jogger (Verb)

Meaning: to move by showing, bumping or jerking

Use: A rough wagon ride that jogged the passengers.

Joint (Noun)

Meaning: place where two pr more parts are joined together

Use: She and her husband have a joint bank account.

Joker (Noun)

Meaning: one who jokes

Use: He is, by nature, a joker, a witty man with a sense of fun.

Jolly (Adjective)

Meaning: jovial merry

Use: He's in quite a jolly mood today.

Jolt (Noun)

Meaning: to shake with jerk

Use: The bus jolted along the road.

Journalism (Noun)

Meaning: the collecting, writing, editing and presenting of news or news articles in newspapers and magazines and in radio. television broadcasts

Use: I want to do degree in Journalism.

Journalize (Verb)

Meaning: enter in journal

Use: His job is only to journalize the things.

Jovial (Adjective)

Meaning: merry

Use: He seems to be in a very jovial mood this morning.

Jubilance (Noun)

Meaning: exultation

Use: He jumps with a feeling of jubilance when he knew he become father.

Judge (Verb)

Meaning: decide cases to form opinion, to estimate to consider

Use: My husband is a judge in Supreme Court.

Judicious (Adjective)

Meaning: exercising sound judgement

Use: The fire fighters made judicious use of flame-retardant foam as the burning airplane skidded along the runway.

Judgment (Noun)

Meaning: the act or process of judging, the formation of an opinion after consideration or deliberation

Use: She showed good judgement in saving her money

Jugular (Adjective)

Meaning: of, relating to

Use: A strategic attack aimed at the enemy's Juglar.

Jumble (Verb)

Meaning: to mix together confusedly, to put together without order

Use: He found an untidy jumble of thing in the drawer.

Junior (Adjective)

Meaning: younger, (one lower in rank)

Use: He is junior to me in the firm.

Junction (Noun)

Meaning: a place at which things joins, (eg railway lines)

Use: There was an accident at the junction of Park Road and School Lane.

Juridical (Adjective)

Meaning: legal of judiciary

Use: Always follow the Juridical rules.

Jurisdiction (Noun)

Meaning: sphere of legal authority

Use: the police have no jurisdiction over foreign bank accounts.

Justice (Noun)

Meaning: fairness or rightness in the treatment of other people

Use: Everyone has a right to Justice.

Jussive (Adjective)

Meaning: expressing

Use: He is not a jussive person.

Justiciable (Adjective)

Meaning: subject to jurisdiction

Use: They have justiciable disputes between them.

Justification (Noun)

Meaning: act of justifying

Use: I knew there was no justification for what I was doing.

Juvenilia (Noun)

Meaning: books etc. written during author's youth

Use: This book was Juvenilia, written in middle period.

Joystick (Noun)

Meaning: a manual control or cursor device, as one attached to a computer or videogame

Use: He is playing game with Joystick not with keyboard.

Juxtapose (Verb)

Meaning: to place side by side

Use: Comedy and tragedy were juxtaposed in the play which was alternately funny and sad.

K

Kangaroo (Noun)

Meaning: any of several herbivorous leaping marsupials of Australia having large powerful hind legs and a long thick tail

Use: The kangaroo is a national symbol of Australia.

Kaleidoscope (Noun)

Meaning: optical toy which being turned shows variety of beautiful forms and colours

Use: We can feel illusions if we see something by kaleidoscope.

Karate (Noun)

Meaning: a traditional Japanese system of unarmed combat, sharp blows and kicks are given to pressure- sensitive points on the body of opponent

Use: Karate was developed in the Ryukyu Kingdom prior to its 19th century by Japan.

Karma (Noun)

Meaning: the effects of a person's actions that determine his destiny in his next incarnation

Use: My Karma ran over your dogma.

Keck (Verb)

Meaning: make sound as if to vomit

Use: Another name of Keck is Cow parsnip.

Keen (Adjective)

Meaning: finely sharpened, as an edge

Use: He used a keen razor for shaving.

Keep (Verb)

Meaning: to continue or persist in (doing something)

Use: We cannot keep several servants any longer.

Keeper (Noun)

Meaning: one who keeps or guard

Use: The Portuguese keeper made one of the most remarkable saves.

Kennel (Noun)

Meaning: an establishment where dogs are bred, trained or boarded

Use: The dog made his kennel in a tree hole.

Kernel (Noun)

Meaning: the central or most important part of anything

Use: His leadership is the kernel of the organisation.

Kettle (Noun)

Meaning: a metal container used to boil liquids

Use: In our Home, we make tea with electric kettle.

Kibble (Noun)

Meaning: hoisting bucket used in mines

Use: we need some more kibble for the labour working in mines.

Kick (Verb)

Meaning: to strike out with force

Use: The powerful rifle kicked upon being fired.

Kid (Adjective)

Meaning: used as a term of familiar address, especially for a young person

Use: Hi, kid! What's up?

Kidnap (Verb)

Meaning: to carry off a person by force, often demanding money in exchange of his safe returns

Use: He is very wealthy and lives in fear of his children being kidnapped.

Kidney (Noun)

Meaning: one of a pair of organs in the body which remove waste matter from the blood and produce Urine

Use: The kidneys of some animals are used as food.

Kill (Verb)

Meaning: to cause the death of

Use: He killed the rats with poison.

Killer (Noun)

Meaning: a person, animal etc. that kills

Use: There is a killer wondering in the village.

Kiln (Noun)

Meaning: a type of large oven for baking bricks, drying grains etc.

Use: In cement factory, Labour use Kiln for drying cement.

Kilt (Noun)

Meaning: a knee - length skirt with deep pleats, usually of a tartan wool

Use: Kilt is a part of the dress for men in the Scottish Highlands.

Kinetic (Adjective)

Meaning: having to do with motion, lively, active

Use: Kinetic energy is energy associated with motion.

Kindle (Verb)

Meaning: to set on fire to inflame

Use: The sunset kindled the skies.

King (Noun)

Meaning: sovereign monarch, King of King (God Emperor)

Use: I have two cards – the ten of spades and the king of diamonds.

Kitchen (Noun)

Meaning: room in which cooking is done

Use: A smell of burning was çoming from the kitchen.

Kith (Noun)

Meaning: Kith & Kin (friends & relatives)

Use: Kith and kin these words are only used in phrases.

Knapsack (Noun)

Meaning: bag of canvas or leather carried on back

Use: He stuffed his laundry into a large bag.

Knavish (Adjective)

Meaning: dishonest

Use: Don't trust on his knavish trick again.

Knob (Noun)

Meaning: hard round protuberance, rounded handle of door

Use: He turned the knob and pushed against the door.

Knock (Adjective)

Meaning: strike against something with blow, to clash, to wander

Use: Knock at my window at eight o'clock and I'll be ready.

Knocker (Noun)

Meaning: iron fastened to door

Use: You pay on the knocker here.

Knotty (Adjective)

Meaning: knotted, difficult

Use: The new management team faces some knotty problems.

Knowable (Adjective)

Meaning: apt to be known

Use: That movie is full with unknowable mysteries of life.

Knowledge (Noun)

Meaning: learning, awareness

Use: She disclaims any knowledge of her husband's business concern.

Knead (Verb)

Meaning: to squeeze, press or rolls with hands

Use: Kneading a painful calf muscle.

Knurled (Adjective)

Meaning: knotted, knobby

Use: He has knurled problems in his life.

Kraal (Noun)

Meaning: enclosure for sheep or cattle

Use: In villages people use kraal to surround stocks of grass.

Koumiss (Noun)

Meaning: fermented liquor from mare's milk

Use: Koumiss is made originally by nomads of central Asia.

Kymograph (Noun)

Meaning: instrument for recording (blood) pressure

Use: Kymograph is generally used by doctors.

Key (Adjective)

Meaning: something crucial for explaining

Use: The key to development is economic integration.

Keyboard (Noun)

Meaning: device consisting of a set of keys use to operate machines

Use: A musical keyboard consists of music keys only.

Keyhole (Noun)

Meaning: the hole in a lock into which a key fits

Use: Insert key into keyhole otherwise you will not be able to open lock.

Keynote (Noun)

Meaning: a prime underlying element or theme

Use: The keynote of the revolution settlement was personal freedom under the law.

Key ring (Noun)

Meaning: a circular ring of metal for holding keys

Use: I bought a new key ring for my keys.

L

Laboratory (Noun)

Meaning: place where scientific experiment are conducted

Use: Sample of her blood was sent to the hospital laboratory for testing.

Labour (Verb)

Meaning: to toil to work hard to strive……

Use: He spends the summer labouring on a building site.

Labyrinth (Noun)

Meaning: a maze, something like a maze

Use: The bill took many months to pass through the labyrinth of congressional approval.

Laconic (Adjective)

Meaning: using few words, especially to the point of seeming rude

Use: The manager's laconic dismissal letter left the fired employees feeling angry and hurt.

Lactiferous (Adjective)

Meaning: yielding milk

Use: In botany, we learnt lactiferous process.

Ladder (Noun)

Meaning: portable, frame with step (rungs) for ascending building

Use: She broke her arm when she fell off a ladder.

Lament (Verb)

Meaning: to mourn

Use: As the snowstorm gained in intensity, Stan lamented his decision that morning to dress in shorts and a T-shirt.

Lampoon (Verb)

Meaning: to satirize, to mock, to parody

Use: The irreverent students mercilessly lampooned their Latin teacher's lisp in a skit at the school talent show.

Languish (Verb)

Meaning: to become weak, listless, depressed

Use: The longer Jill remained unemployed, the more she languished and the less likely it became that she would find another job.

Lance (Noun)

Meaning: spear with long handle

Use: The doctor lanced the boil on my neck.

Language (Noun)

Meaning: faculty of human speech, words and their use by nation style of expression.

Use: she is very good at learning languages.

Laniferous (Adjective)

Meaning: wool

Use: In Sikkim, I saw laniferous sheep.

Lapel (Noun)

Meaning: inner fold on breast of coat

Use: Narrow lapels are in fashion.

Lapicide (Noun)

Meaning: one who cuts stones, inscription on stone

Use: Her job is to lapicide and create designs on hill.

Lapse (Verb)

Meaning: to slip, to glide, decline, slight error, passing away

Use: She allowed her membership to lapse after the first year.

Larder (Noun)

Meaning: room for keeping provision

Use: The larder was stocked with tasty home-made jams and chutneys.

Largesse (Noun)

Meaning: gift, donation

Use: The president has been traveling around the country distributing largesse.

Lasque (Noun)

Meaning: ill-formed diamond

Use: Don't wear that necklace, it looks lasque.

Last (Verb)

Meaning: to continue to exist, to endure……

Use: He was the last guest to leave.

Lather (Noun)

Meaning: froth of soap and water

Use: The students were in a lather over the proposed restrictions.

Latitude (Noun)

Meaning: freedom from narrowness, extent, comprehensiveness, angular distance from equator

Use: What is the latitude of Sikkim?

Latent (Adjective)

Meaning: present but not visible or apparent, potential

Use: A Photographic image is latent in a piece of exposed film. It's there. But you can't see it until the film is developed.

Laud (Verb)

Meaning: to praise, to applaud, to extol, to celebrate

Use: The bank manager lauded the hero who trapped the escaping robber.

Laudable (Adjective)

Meaning: worthy of praise

Use: One of her less laudable characteristics was her jealousy.

Launder (Verb)

Meaning: to wash and iron

Use: She couldn't go to the party as she had to launder the sheets.

Lavatory (Noun)

Meaning: place of washing hand & face

Use: Show him the way to lavatory.

Lavish (Adjective)

Meaning: wasteful, extravagant abundant

Use: The critics were lavish with their praise.

Lawful (Adjective)

Meaning: rightful

Use: It's a lawful duty of doctors to treat their patients best.

Lead (Noun)

Meaning: heavy metal, stick of graphite used in pencils

Use: He warned that a pay rise would lead to job cuts.

League (Noun)

Meaning: confederation union distance of about 3 miles

Use: Her success has taken her out of my league.

Lease (Noun)

Meaning: contract of house, land for limited period

Use: He leases the land from the local council.

Ledger (Noun)

Meaning: book of account

Use: He kept detailed records in an accounts ledger.

Legacy (Noun)

Meaning: something handed down from the past, a bequest

Use: The legacy of the corrupt administration was chaos, bankruptcy and despair.

Leghorn (Noun)

Meaning: small domestic fowl

Use: Leghorn is an Italian variety of wheat.

Legislate (Verb)

Meaning: to make laws

Use: The government plan to legislate against the import of foreign cars.

Lemon (Noun)

Meaning: Sour-juiced fruit like orange

Use: In summer I like lemon juice.

Lentil (Noun)

Meaning: kind of bean

Use: Lentil is found in plants of southwest Asia.

Leper (Noun)

Meaning: one afflicted with leprosy

Use: The article branded her a social leper.

Lessor (Noun)

Meaning: one who grants lease

Use: He is the lessor of a chain of restaurants.

Leverage (Noun)

Meaning: power gained by using lever

Use: His positions affords him the leverage to get things done through committees.

Lethargy (Noun)

Meaning: sluggishness, laziness, drowsiness, indifference

Use: The couch potato had fallen into a state of such total lethargy that he never moved except to channels or get another bag of Doritos from the kitchen.

Levigation (Noun)

Meaning: act of levigating

Use: Levigation process can make things smooth.

Liasison (Noun)

Meaning: unlawful connection between man and woman

Use: They like their liasison relation.

Libel (Noun)

Meaning: a written or published falsehood that injures the reputation of, or defames, someone

Use: Slander is just like libel except that it is spoken instead of written. To slander someone is to say something untrue that injures that person's reputation

Liberty (Noun)

Meaning: freedom, unrestrained enjoyment of natural rights, privilege

Use: He ordered that all prisoners should be given their liberty.

Licensee (Noun)

Meaning: one who hold license

Use: He is a licensee of Alcoholic drinks.

Ligament (Noun)

Meaning: fibrous tissue connecting bones at joints

Use: She pulled a ligament in her knee when she fell.

Lighten (Verb)

Meaning: to shed light, to reduce weight of

Use: He felt the need to lighten the atmosphere.

Limit (Noun)

Meaning: boundary

Use: We must limit the amount of time we spend on this work.

Limpid (Adjcctive)

Meaning: clear, pure

Use: The speech was a model of its kind-limpid and unaffected.

Litigate (Verb)

Meaning: to try in court, to engage in legal proceedings

Use: When the company was unable to recover its money outside of court, its only option was to litigate.

Loquacious (Adjective)

Meaning: talking a lot or too much

Use: The child was surprisingly loquacious for one so small.

Lucid (Adjective)

Meaning: clear, easy to understand

Use: The professor's explanation of the theory of relativity was so astonishingly lucid that even I could understand it.

Lugubrious (Adjective)

Meaning: exaggerated mournful

Use: Harish's lugubrious eulogy at the funeral of his mother eventually made everyone start giggling.

Luminous (Adjective)

Meaning: giving off light, glowing, bright

Use: The moon was a luminous disk in the cloudy nighttime sky.

Lyric (Adjective)

Meaning: pertaining to lyre, poetic, musical, song expressive of poem's emotions

Use: The tune is good, but I don't like the lyrics.

M

Machinery (Noun)

Meaning: machines in general, system of machines, means for given purpose

Use: Farmers import most of their machinery and materials.

Machination (Noun)

Meaning: scheming activity for an evil purpose

Use: The ruthless machinations of the mobsters left a trail of blood and bodies.

Magnesium (Noun)

Meaning: kind of white metal

Use: Magnesium occurs naturally as periclase.

Magnanimous (Adjective)

Meaning: forgiving, noble in spirit, generous

Use: The boxer was magnanimous in defeat, telling the sports reporters that his opponent had simply been too talented for him to beat.

Magnate (Noun)

Meaning: a rich, powerful or very successful business-person

Use: John D. Rockefeller was a magnate who was never too busy to give a shoeshine boy a dime for his troubles.

Majority (Noun)

Meaning: greater number, full age

Use: The majority of our customers come from out of town.

Malpractice (Noun)

Meaning: improper conduct

Use: that doctor do malpractice.

Malaise (Noun)

Meaning: feeling uneasy or queasy

Use: Malaise descended on the calculus class when the teacher announced a quiz.

Malfeasance (Noun)

Meaning: an illegal act, especially by a public official

Use: President Ford officially pardoned former president Nixon before the latter could be convicted of any malfeasance.

Malinger (Verb)

Meaning: to pretend to be sick to avoid doing work

Use: Puneet always malingered when it was his turn to clean up the house.

Malleable (Adjective)

Meaning: easy to shape or bend

Use: Modelling clay is very malleable.

Mandatory (Noun)

Meaning: conveying mandate

Use: Attendance at the meeting is mandatory.

Manner (Noun)

Meaning: way in which thing is done, mode, fashion, style

Use: She greeted me in a friendly manner.

Manufacture (Noun)

Meaning: making of goods on large scale by machinery

Use: The firm manufactures cars at the rate of two hundred per day.

Manifest (Adjective)

Meaning: visible, evident

Use: Rajesh's anger at us was manifest: you could see it in his expression and hear it in his voice.

Mandate (Noun)

Meaning: a command or authorization to do something, the will of the voters as expressed by the results of an election

Use: The newly elected president felt that the landslide vote had given him a mandate to do whatever he wanted to do.

Manifesto (Noun)

Meaning: a public declaration of beliefs or principles, usually political ones

Use: Ajay's article about the election was less a piece of reporting than a manifesto of his political views.

Marshal (Verb)

Meaning: to arrange in order, to gather together for the purpose of doing something

Use: The statistician marshaled his facts before making his presentation.

Martial (Adjective)

Meaning: warlike, having to do with combat

Use: The parade of soldiers was martial in tone. The soldiers carried rifles and were followed by a formation of tanks.

Matriculate (Verb)

Meaning: to enroll, especially at a college

Use: Brijesh told everyone that he was going to Shimla, but when he actually matriculated it was at the local junior college.

Margin (Noun)

Meaning: edge, border

Use: Please write your comments in the margin.

Maudlin (Adjective)

Meaning: silly and sentimental

Use: The high school reunion grew more and more maudlin as the participants had more and more to drink.

Maunder (Verb)

Meaning: to move listlessly

Use: This depressed patient does not maunder.

Maverick (Noun)

Meaning: a nonconformist, a rebel

Use: The political scientist was an intellectual maverick. Most of his theories had no followers except himself.

Maxim (Noun)

Meaning: a fundamental principle, an old saying

Use: We always tried to live our lives according to the maxim that it is better to give than to receive.

Mechanism – (Noun)

Meaning: construction of machine

Use: The heat-producing mechanism will switch itself on automatically.

Mediate (Verb)

Meaning: to help settle differences

Use: Ronit carried messages back and forth between the divorcing husband and wife in the hope of mediating their differences.

Melanism (Noun)

Meaning: blackness of skin

Use: He is suffering from melanism

Memorial (Adjective)

Meaning: (something) serving to preserve memory, public petition, monument or record

Use: The museum will serve as a memorial to all those who died.

Mendacious (Adjective)

Meaning: lying, dishonest

Use: The jury saw through the mendacious witness and convicted the defendant.

Mendicant (Noun)

Meaning: a beggar

Use: The presence of thousands of mendicants in every urban area is a sad commentary on our national priorities.

Mercerize (Verb)

Meaning: to treat cotton cloth with silky gloss

Use: In mercerize Cotton cloth with sodium hydroxide.

Meritorious (Adjective)

Meaning: deserving

Use: I had been promoted for gallant and meritorious service.

Mercenary (Noun)

Meaning: a hired soldier, someone who will do anything for money

Use: If an army can't find enough volunteers or draftees, it will sometimes hire mercenaries.

Mercurial (Adjective)

Meaning: emotionally unpredictable, rapidly changing in mood

Use: A person with a mercurial personality is one who changes rapidly and unpredictably between one mood and another.

Metamorphosis (Noun)

Meaning: a magical change in form, a striking or sudden change

Use: When the magician passed his want over Sheerin's head, she underwent a bizarre metamorphosis. She turned into a hamster.

Microcosm (Noun)

Meaning: the world in miniature

Use: To cosmos is the heaven, cosmopolitan means worldly and a microcosm is a miniature version of the world. All three words are related.

Microscope (Noun)

Meaning: optical instrument for magnifying objects

Use: Germs are very small, and can only be seen with the aid of a microscope.

Micturition (Noun)

Meaning: frequent desire to make water

Use: Micturition is a natural body process.

Migrant (Noun)

Meaning: migratory animal or bird

Use: When seasons changes, many migrant birds came to India.

Mileage (Noun)

Meaning: rate, etc. per mile

Use: This tire will give very good mileage.

Milieu (Noun)

Meaning: environment; surroundings

Use: The farmer on vacation in the big city felt out of his milieu.

Millennial (Noun)

Meaning: thousand into thousand

Use: He spent many millennial on this project.

Mindful (Adjective)

Meaning: attentive, careful

Use: We must be mindful of the consequences of selfishness.

Miniature (Noun)

Meaning: small sized painting

Use: The farm has been selling miniature roses since 1970.

Minster (Noun)

Meaning: cathedral

Use: Minster is also known as a monastery church.

Minuscule (Adjective)

Meaning: very tiny

Use: Harit's salary was minuscule, but the benefits were pretty good. He got to sit next to the refrigerator and eat all day long.

Miracle (Noun)

Meaning: supernatural event, marvel

Use: It's a miracle he wasn't killed in the plane crush.

Misapply (Verb)

Meaning: to put to wrong use

Use: The law has been misapplied.

Misconduct (Noun)

Meaning: Ill behaviour

Use: He was dismissed from his job for gross misconduct.

Miserable (Adjective)

Meaning: poor pitiable, wretched

Use: The house was in a miserable condition.

Misgovern (Verb)

Meaning: govern badly

Use: He is misgoverning the nation.

Misinterpret (Verb)

Meaning: to explain wrongly

Use: The Prince's word had been misinterpreted.

Misprint (Verb)

Meaning: print incorrectly

Use: This book is full of misprints.

Mission (Noun)

Meaning: sending out of number of person abroad entrusted with special work

Use: His mission was to seek help.

Mistrust (Noun)

Meaning: want of trust

Use: You should mistrust all journalists.

Mitigate (Verb)

Meaning: to moderate the effect of something

Use: The sense of imminent disaster was mitigated by the guide's calm behaviour and easy smile.

Momentous (Adjective)

Meaning: important

Use: I took the momentous decision to send in the troops.

Monster (Noun)

Meaning: imaginary frightful animal or person, brutal fellow, something of extraordinary

Use: The film will be a monster hit.

Moquette (Noun)

Meaning: wool, hemp etc. for making carpet

Use: She want to make wallpaper with moquette.

Mortification (Noun)

Meaning: self-denial

Use: The chairman tried to hide his mortification.

Morose (Adjective)

Meaning: gloomy, sullen

Use: Loutise was always so morose about everything that she was never any fun to be with.

Mortify (Verb)

Meaning: to humiliate

Use: We had a mortifying experience at the opera; when Stanley sneezed, the entire orchestra stopped playing and stared at him for several minutes.

Motionless (Adjective)

Meaning: without motion

Use: He stood their motionless.

Moustache (Noun)

Meaning: hair on upper lip of man

Use: The young man has grown a moustache.

Multiplex (Adjective)

Meaning: manifold

Use: The whole complex and multiplex details of the noble science of dinner.

Mummer (Noun)

Meaning: play-actor in festival shows

Use: He is a mummer actor.

Mundane (Adjective)

Meaning: ordinary, pretty boring, not heavenly and eternal

Use: My day was filled with mundane chores. I mowed the lawn, did the laundry, fed the dog and fed the dog to the gorilla.

Munificent (Adjective)

Meaning: very generous, lavish

Use: The munificent millionaire gave lots of money to any charity that came to him with a request.

Mural (Adjective)

Meaning: pertaining to walls

Use: That painting is a mural.

Muster (Verb)

Meaning: to gather or be gathered together

Use: He mustered his energy for a final effort.

Mutual (Adjective)

Meaning: pertaining to two or more person alike

Use: Their dislikes was mutual.

Myopia (Adjective)

Meaning: nearsightedness, lack of foresight

Use: The worker's dissatisfaction was inflamed by management's myopia on the subject of wages.

Myriad (Noun)

Meaning: a huge number

Use: A country sky on a clear night is filled with a myriad of stars.

Mystery (Noun)

Meaning: something hidden or unintelligible

Use: The woman in the photograph is a mystery.

Myth (Noun)

Meaning: story handed down from very ancient times regarding religious beliefs

Use: He is a star whose fame turned into a myth.

Mythological (Adjective)

Meaning: pertaining to mythology

Use: The mythological beast that was part lion, lion goat.

Mythoplasm (Noun)

Meaning: essence of myths

Use: He is full of mythoplasm.

N

Naphtha (Noun)

Meaning: kind of inflammable oil got from Coal etc.

Use: Naphtha is usually flammable and used as an ingredient in gasoline.

Narcissism (Noun)

Meaning: excessive love of one's body or one-self

Use: The selfish students were bound up in narcissistic concerns and gave no thought to other people.

Narration (Noun)

Meaning: act of narrating

Use: The play is an autobiographical journey with song, dialogue and narration.

Nasal (Adjective)

Meaning: pertaining to nose

Use: He use nasal voice.

Nationality (Noun)

Meaning: being member of nation

Use: Different nationalities are found in this city.

Natural (Adjective)

Meaning: produced by nature

Use: Wild animals are happier in their natural state than in zoo.

Naturalist (Noun)

Meaning: student of biology

Use: Dr Prabhakar is a professional naturalist and author.

Navicular (Adjective)

Meaning: boat shaped

Use: His house is navicular in shape.

Nebula (Noun)

Meaning: little cloudiness of sight

Use: I saw a reflection of nebula in sky.

Nebulous (Adjective)

Meaning: vague, hazy, indistinct

Use: The community's boundaries are somewhat nebulous, where they are depends on whom you ask.

Necessary (Noun)

Meaning: indispensable thing

Use: Food is one of the necessities of life.

Nectar (Noun)

Meaning: very delicious drink

Use: Her words are nector to me.

Needle (Noun)

Meaning: sharp pointed thin wire of steel for sewing

Use: She could see that she had needled him with her constant questions.

Nefarious (Adjective)

Meaning: evil, flagrantly wicked

Use: The convicted murderer had committed a myriad of nefarious acts.

Negation (Noun)

Meaning: denial, refusal

Use: She shook her head in a gesture of negation.

Neighbour (Noun)

Meaning: person living near by

Use: He lives somewhere in the neighbourhood of the station.

Neologism (Noun)

Meaning: new word or phrase, a new usage of a word

Use: Pedants don't like neologisms. They like the words we already have. But at one time every word was a neologism. Someone somewhere had to be the first to use it.

Nephology (Noun)

Meaning: study of clouds

Use: The branch of nephrology deals with clouds.

Nepotism (Noun)

Meaning: showing favouritism to friends or family in business or politics

Use: Leander had no business acumen, so he was counting on nepotism when he married the boss's daughter.

Nervous (Adjective)

Meaning: pertaining to excite

Use: I get very nervous when I'm in the house alone at night.

Nettle (Noun)

Meaning: stinging plant

Use: I instantly regretted my remark, because it obviously nettled him.

Neutral (Adjective)

Meaning: taking part on neither side

Use: A neutral country was asked to help settle the dispute.

News (Noun)

Meaning: fresh tidings

Use: She is no longer news in the film world.

Nickel (Noun)

Meaning: silvery white metal

Use: Millerite is a yellow mineral consisting of nickel sulfide.

Nidify (Verb)

Meaning: to build nest

Use: Birds do nidify to live.

Nightingale (Noun)

Meaning: small singing bird, someone who has sweet voice

Use: Lata Mangeshkar is known as the nightingale of India.

Nihilism (Noun)

Meaning: the belief that there are no values or morals in the universe

Use: A nihilist does not believe in any objective standards of right or wrong.

Nitre (Noun)

Meaning: saltpetre

Use: Nitre is used in fertilizers to make soil fertile.

Noble (Adjective)

Meaning: grand, impressive

Use: The nobbles planned to murder the king.

Nominal (Adjective)

Meaning: in name only, insignificant, A-OK (during rocket launches)

Use: Bert was the nominal Chairman of the committee, but Sue was really the one who ran things.

Nomadic (Adjective)

Meaning: wandering about

Use: The nomadic tribes of the western Sahara.

Nonchalance (Noun)

Meaning: indifference

Use: He walked in with exaggerated nonchalance, his hands in his pockets.

Normal (Adjective)

Meaning: ordinary, usual

Use: He was behaving quite normally yesterday.

Nostalgia (Noun)

Meaning: sentimental longing for the past, homesickness

Use: Some people who don't remember what the decade was really like feel a misplaced nostalgia for the 1950s.

Notation (Noun)

Meaning: representing numbers

Use: He was checking

Notice (Noun)

Meaning: intimation

Use: He had to make the speech at very short notice when his boss suddenly fell ill.

Notorious (Adjective)

Meaning: famous for something bad

Use: A well-known actor is famous. A well-known criminal is notorious.

Nourish (Verb)

Meaning: to nurture

Use: The food that mother eats nourishes both her and her baby.

Novel (Adjective)

Meaning: new, original

Use: Ray had a novel approach to homework. He didn't do it. Ray failed geometry as a result of this novelty.

Noxious (Adjective)

Meaning: harmful, offensive

Use: Smoking is a noxious habit in every sense.

Nuance (Noun)

Meaning: a subtle difference or distinction

Use: The artist's best work explored the nuance between darkness and deep shadow.

Nucleus (Noun)

Meaning: central part of thing

Use: The Civic Movement could be the nucleus of a centrist party of the future.

Nuisance (Noun)

Meaning: anything offensive or annoying

Use: That child is a terrible nuisance.

Numismatics (Noun)

Meaning: study of coins and medals

Use: She is most interesting in numismatics.

Nutrient (Noun)

Meaning: providing nourishment

Use: Give nutrient solution to baby.

Nuzzle (Verb)

Meaning: to sniff

Use: The dog came and nuzzled up against me.

Nymph (Noun)

Meaning: semi divine goddess

Use: Nymph can change anyone's life.

Nystagmus (Noun)

Meaning: kind of eye disease

Use: He is suffering from nystagmus.

O

Oath (Noun)

Meaning: solemn affirmation to god

Use: He swore an oath to support king.

Obdurate (Adjective)

Meaning: stubborn and insensitive

Use: The child begged and begged to have a bubble-gum machine installed in his bedroom, but his parents were obdurate in their insistence that he have a soft-drink machine instead

Obesity (Noun)

Meaning: fatness

Use: Excessive consumption of sugar and fat leads to obesity.

Obfuscate (Verb)

Meaning: to darken, to confuse, to make confusing

Use: People had hoped the spokesman would elucidate the issue. But he only obfuscated the issue further

Objection (Noun)

Meaning: expression of disapproval

Use: This objection has obviously been dropped.

Objector (Noun)

Meaning: one who objects

Use: He is the only objector of this drama.

Oblige (Verb)

Meaning: kindness to

Use: The police obliged him to leave.

Oblique (Adjective)

Meaning: indirect, at an angle

Use: In geometry, lines are said to be oblique if they are neither parallel nor perpendicular to each other. The word has a related meaning outside of mathematics.

Oblivion (Noun)

Meaning: total forgetfulness, the state of being forgotten

Use: A few of the young actors would find face, but most were headed for oblivion.

Obscure (Adjective)

Meaning: unknown, hard to understand, dark

Use: The artist was so obscure that even his parents had trouble remembering his name.

Obscenity (Noun)

Meaning: lewdness

Use: They shouted obscenities at us as we passed.

Obsequious (Adjective)

Meaning: fawning, subservient, sucking up to

Use: Ann's assistant was so obsequious that she could never tell what he really thought about anything.

Observation (Noun)

Meaning: perception

Use: This book contains observations about the nature of addiction.

Obstinate (Adjective)

Meaning: stubborn

Use: He is obstinate and determined and will not give up.

Obstruction (Noun)

Meaning: hindrance

Use: The boy was suffering from a bowel obstruction.

Obverse (Adjective)

Meaning: turned towards one

Use: The obverse of "Every act is predictable" is "No act is unpredictable."

Occupancy (Noun)

Meaning: act or right of holding

Use: Prices given are for a single occupancy of a standard room.

Occurrence (Noun)

Meaning: incidents

Use: Traffic jams are now a daily occurrence.

Octagon (Noun)

Meaning: plane of figure of eight sides

Use: This room has octagon shape.

Odourous (Adjective)

Meaning: fragrant

Use: I like the odourous air of the orchard.

Offend (Verb)

Meaning: to make angry

Use: The smell of cigar smoke offends me.

Official (Adjective)

Meaning: pertaining to office

Use: An official announcement is expected later today.

Olympian (Adjective)

Meaning: superior magnificent

Use: He has Olympian power.

Omission (Noun)

Meaning: neglect

Use: There is one noticeable omission in your article.

Omnipotent (Adjective)

Meaning: all – powerful.

Use: The omnipotent power of god.

Opaque (Adjective)

Meaning: impossible to see through, impossible to understand

Use: We tried to figure out what Horace was thinking, but his expression was opaque. It revealed nothing.

Opening (Noun)

Meaning: commencement

Use: We don't have any openings just now, but we'll call you later.

Operative (Adjective)

Meaning: artisan

Use: In an automated car plant there is not a human operative to be seen.

Opinion (Noun)

Meaning: what one believes or supposes

Use: He wanted a second opinion on his illness.

Opposition (Adjective)

Meaning: act of opposing

Use: The team inflicted a crushing defeat on the opposition.

Oppressive (Adjective)

Meaning: tyrannical

Use: The oppressive afternoon heat had quite tired him out.

Optimist (Noun)

Meaning: one who believes that whatever happens is for best

Use: He is an optimist.

Opulent (Adjective)

Meaning: luxurious

Use: Everything in the opulent palace was made of gold, except the toilet paper holder, which was made of platinum.

Oral (Adjective)

Meaning: spoken, verbal

Use: All students have to take a written and oral examination.

Oratory (Noun)

Meaning: eloquence

Use: Neither candidate is noted for oratory or political skill.

Ordinance (Noun)

Meaning: quassi-law issued by an authority

Use: Ordinances that restrict building development,

Organisation (Noun)

Meaning: society for some special objects

Use: Most of the funds are provided by voluntary organisations.

Ornamentation (Noun)

Meaning: decoration

Use: The décor was functional and free of ornamentation.

Orpiment (Noun)

Meaning: yellow mineral

Use: Orpiment is used as pigment.

Oscitant (Adjective)

Meaning: yawning, sleeping

Use: He always oscitant while work.

Ostentatious (Adjective)

Meaning: excessively conspicuous, showing off

Use: The young lawyer had ostentatiously hung his Harvard diploma on the door to his office.

Ostensible (Adjective)

Meaning: outwardly showing

Use: Illness was the ostensible reason for his absence, but in fact he was just lazy.

Otter (Noun)

Meaning: kind of weasel living on fish

Use: I saw many beautiful otter in river.

Outcome (Noun)

Meaning: result or consequences

Use: What was the outcome of your discussion?

Outlast (Verb)

Meaning: to last longer than

Use: Artificial flowers outlast natural flowers, but they don't appear too pleasing.

Outrageous (Adjective)

Meaning: furious, violent

Use: Charge for long-distance telephone calls are absolutely outrageous.

Ovation (Noun)

Meaning: public applause

Use: They gave the president a standing ovation.

Overbid (Verb)

Meaning: to bid more than value

Use: He overbid this necklace.

Oyster (Noun)

Meaning: kind of shell-fish

Use: The world is his oyster.

Ozone (Noun)

Meaning: condensed form of oxygen

Use: Earth is covered with ozone layer.

P

Pacify (Verb)

Meaning: to calm someone down, to placate

Use: A parent gives a baby a pacifier to pacify him or her.

Painstaking (Adjective)

Meaning: extremely careful, taking pains

Use: We made a painstaking effort to move the piano without harming it.

Palliate (Verb)

Meaning: to relieve or alleviate something without getting rid of the problem, to assuage, to mitigate

Use: You take aspirin in the hope that it will palliate your headache. Aspirin is a palliative.

Palpable (Adjective)

Meaning: capable of being touched, obvious, tangible

Use: The tumor was palpable. The doctor could feel it with his finger.

Paltry (Adjective)

Meaning: insignificant, worthless

Use: The lawyer's efforts in our behalf were paltry; they didn't add up to anything.

Panacea (Noun)

Meaning: something that cures everything

Use: The administration seemed to believe that a tax cut would be a panacea for the country's economic ills.

Parody (Noun)

Meaning: a satirical imitation

Use: At the talent show the girls sang a terrible parody of a Beatles song called I Want to Hold Your Foot.

Parsimonious (Adjective)

Meaning: stingy

Use: The old widow was so parsimonious that she hung used teabags out to dry on her clothesline so that she would be able to use them again.

Partisan (Noun)

Meaning: one who supports a particular person, cause or idea

Use: The mountain village was attacked by partisans of the rebel chieftain.

Patent (Adjective)

Meaning: obvious

Use: To say that the earth is flat is a patent absurdity, since the world is obviously spherical.

Paternal (Adjective)

Meaning: fatherly, father like

Use: Freud is paternal toward his niece.

Pathology (Noun)

Meaning: the science of disease

Use: Pathology is the science or study of diseases, but not necessarily in the medical sense.

Patrician (Noun)

Meaning: a person of noble birth, an aristocrat

Use: Mr. Anderson was a patrician, and he was never truly happy unless his place at the dinner table was set with at least half a dozen forks.

Paucity (Noun)

Meaning: scarcity

Use: There was a paucity of fresh vegetables at the supermarket so we had to buy frozen ones.

Peccadillo (Noun)

Meaning: a minor offence

Use: The smiling defendant acted as though first-degree murder were a mere peccadillo rather than a hideous crime.

Pedantic (Adjective)

Meaning: boringly scholarly or academic

Use: The discussion quickly turned pedantic as each participant tried to sound more learned than all others.

Pejorative (Adjective)

Meaning: negative, disparaging

Use: Abe's description of the college as a pretty good school was unintentionally pejorative.

Pedestrian (Adjective)

Meaning: unimaginative, banal, those who walk in the streets

Use: Mary Anne said the young artist's work was brilliant, but I found it to be pedestrian. I've seen better paintings in kindergarten classrooms.

Penitent (Adjective)

Meaning: sorry, repentant, contrite

Use: Julie was penitent when Hank explained how much pain she had caused him.

Pensive (Adjective)

Meaning: thoughtful and sad

Use: Norton became suddenly pensive when Jack mentioned his dead father. up by shooting off a few firecrackers in the living room.

Peremptory (Adjective)

Meaning: final, categorical, dictatorial

Use: Someone who is peremptory says or does something without giving anyone a chance to dispute it.

Perfunctory (Adjective)

Meaning: unenthusiastic, careless

Use: Lilly made a couple of perfunctory attempts at answering the questions on the test, but then he put down his pencil and his head and slept until the end of the period.

Periphery (Noun)

Meaning: the outside edge of something

Use: Jay never got involved in any of our activities. He was always at the periphery.

Peripatetic (Adjective)

Meaning: wandering, travelling continually, itinerant

Use: Groupies are a peripatetic bunch, traveling from concert to concert to follow their favourite rock stars.

Perquisite (Noun)

Meaning: a privilege that goes along with a job, a perk

Use: Free access to a photocopier is a perquisite of most office jobs.

Pernicious (Adjective)

Meaning: deadly, extremely evil

Use: The drug dealers conducted their pernicious business on every street corner in the city.

Perturb (Verb)

Meaning: to disturb greatly

Use: Rudolph's mother was perturbed by his aberrant behaviour at the dinner table. Rudolph's father was not bothered. Nothing bothered Rudolph Sr. He was imperturbable.

Pertinent (Adjective)

Meaning: relevant, dealing with the matter at hand

Use: The suspect said that he was just borrowing the jewelry for a costume ball. The cop said he did not think that was pertinent.

Peruse (Verb)

Meaning: to read carefully

Use: The lawyer perused the contract for many hours, looking for a loophole that would enable his client to back out of the deal.

Pervade (Verb)

Meaning: to spread throughout

Use: A terrible smell pervaded the 'apartment building after the sewer main exploded.

Philanthropy (Noun)

Meaning: love of mankind, especially by doing good deeds

Use: A charity is a philanthropic institution.

Pious (Adjective)

Meaning: reverent or devout, outwardly (and sometimes falsely) reverent or devout, hypocritical

Use: This is a sometimes confusing word with meanings that are very nearly opposite to each other.

Pivotal (Adjective)

Meaning: crucial

Use: A pivotal member of a committee is crucial or extremely important member of a committee.

Placate (Verb)

Meaning: to pacify, to appease, to soothe

Use: The tribe placated the angry volcano by tossing a few teenagers into the raging crater.

Plaintive (Adjective)

Meaning: expressing sadness or sorrow

Use: The chilly autumn weather made the little bird's song seem plaintive.

Platitude (Noun)

Meaning: a dull or trite remark, a cliché

Use: The principal thinks he is a great orator, but his loud, boring speech was full of platitudes.

Plebian (Adjective)

Meaning: common, vulgar, low class, bourgeois

Use: Sarah refused to eat frozen dinners, saying they were too plebian for her discriminating palate.

Poignant (Adjective)

Meaning: painfully emotional; extremely moving; sharp or astute

Use: A poignant scene is one that is so emotional or moving that it is almost painful to watch.

Plethora (Noun)

Meaning: an excess

Use: We ate a plethora of candy on Halloween and a plethora of turkey on Thanksgiving.

Polemic (Noun)

Meaning: a powerful argument made in refutation of something

Use: The book was a convincing polemic that revealed the fraud at the heart of the large corporation.

Polarize (Verb)

Meaning: to break up into opposing factions or groupings

Use: The increasingly acrimonious debate between the two candidates polarized the political party.

Portent (Noun)

Meaning: an omen; a sign of something coming in the future

Use: The distant rumbling we heard this morning was a portent of the thunderstorm that hit our area this afternoon.

Ponderous (Adjective)

Meaning: so large as to be clumsy; massive; dull

Use: The wedding cake was a ponderous blob of icing and jelly beans.

Postulate (Noun)

Meaning: something accepted as true without proof; an axiom

Use: Sherlock Holmes rarely postulated things, waiting for evidence before he made up his mind.

Pragmatic (Adjective)

Meaning: practical; down to earth; based on experience rather than theory

Use: Erecting a gigantic dome of gold over our house would have been the ideal solution to the leak in our roof, but the small size of our bank account forced us to be pragmatic. We patched the hole with a dab of tar instead.

Precedent (Noun)

Meaning: an earlier example or model of something

Use: To be unprecedented is to have no precedent, to be something entirely new. George's consumption of 10,677 hot dogs was unprecedented. No one had ever eaten so many hot dogs before.

Precept (Noun)

Meaning: a rule to live by, a principle establishing a certain kind of action or behaviour; a maxim

Use: Love the neighbour is a precept we have sometimes found difficult to follow.

Precipitate (Verb)

Meaning: to cause to happen abruptly

Use: A panic among investors precipitated last Monday's crisis in the stock market.

Preclude (Verb)

Meaning: to prevent something from ever happening

Use: Ann feared that her abysmal academic career might preclude her becoming a brain surgeon.

Precursor (Noun)

Meaning: forerunner; something that goes before and anticipates or paves the way for whatever it is that follows

Use: The arrival of a million-dollar check in the mail might very well be the precursor of a brand-new car.

Predilection (Noun)

Meaning: a natural preference for something

Use: The impatient judge had a predilection for well-prepared lawyers who said what they meant and didn't waste his time.

Preeminent (Adjective)

Meaning: better than anyone else; outstanding; supreme

Use: The nation's preeminent harpsichordist would be the best harpsichordist in the nation.

Preempt (Verb)

Meaning: to seize something by prior right

Use: When the air force launched a preemptive strike against the missile base, the air force was attacking the missiles in order to prevent the missiles from attacking the air force.

Premise (Noun)

Meaning: an assumption; the basis for a conclusion

Use: In deciding to eat all the ice cream in the freezer, my premise was that if I didn't do it, you would.

Prepossess (Verb)

Meaning: to preoccupy, to influence beforehand or prejudice, to make a good impression on beforehand

Use: When a person is prepossessed by an idea, he or she can't get it out of his or her mind.

Prerogative (Noun)

Meaning: right or privilege connected exclusively with a position, a person, a class, a nation, or some other group or classification

Use: Sentencing people to death is a prerogative of Kings and Queens.

Prevail (Verb)

Meaning: to triumph, to overcome rivals, (with on, upon, or with) to persuade

Use: When justice prevails, it means that good defeats evil.

Pristine (Adjective)

Meaning: original, unspoiled, pure

Use: An antique in pristine condition is one that hasn't been polluted.

Prodigal (Adjective)

Meaning: wastefully extravagant

Use: The young artist was prodigal with his talents, wasting time and energy on greeting cards that might have been devoted to serious paintings.

Prodigious (Adjective)

Meaning: extraordinary, enormous

Use: The little boy caught a prodigious fish. It was ten times his size and might more easily have caught him had their situations been reversed.

Prodigy (Noun)

Meaning: an extremely talented child, an extraordinary accomplishment or occurrence

Use: The three-year-old prodigy could play all of Beethoven and most of Brahms on his harmonica.

Profane (Adjective)

Meaning: not having to do with religion, irreverent, blasphemous

Use: Profane is the opposite of sacred.

Profess (Verb)

Meaning: to declare, to declare falsely or pretend

Use: Jason professed to teach himself calculus. He declared that he was going to do it.

Proficient (Adjective)

Meaning: thoroughly competent, skillful, very good (at something)

Use: Jerry was a proficient cabinetmaker. He could make a cabinet that would make you sit back and say: Now, there's a cabinet.

Profligate (Adjective)

Meaning: extravagantly wasteful, and, usually, wildly immoral

Use: The young heir was profligate with his fortune, spending millions on champagne and racehorses.

Profound (Adjective)

Meaning: deep (in several senses)

Use: To say something profound is to say something deeply intelligent or discerning.

Proletariat (Noun)

Meaning: the industrial working class

Use: The proletariat is the laboring class or blue-collar workers or people who roll up their shirt sleeves to do an honest day's work.

Proliferate (Verb)

Meaning: to spread or grow rapidly

Use: Honey bees proliferated when we filled out yard with flowering plants.

Prolific (Adjective)

Meaning: abundantly productive, fruitful or fertile

Use: The old man had been extraordinarily prolific. He had thirty children and more than one hundred grandchildren.

Promulgate (Verb)

Meaning: to proclaim, to publicly or formally declare something

Use: The principal promulgated a new dress code over the loudspeaker system: red, green, yellow and blue were the only permissible artificial hair colours.

Propensity (Noun)

Meaning: a natural inclination or tendency, a predilection

Use: Jyoti has a propensity for saying stupid things. Every time she opens her mouth, something stupid comes out.

Propitious (Adjective)

Meaning: marked by favourable signs or conditions

Use: Rush hour is not a propitious time to drive into the city.

Proprietary (Adjective)

Meaning: characteristic of an owner of property, constituting property

Use: To take a proprietary interest in something is to act as though you own it.

Propriety (Noun)

Meaning: properness, good manners

Use: The old lady viewed the little girl's failure to curtsy as a flagrant breach of propriety. She did not approve of or countenance such improprieties.

Prosaic (Adjective)

Meaning: dull, unimaginative, like prose (as opposed to poetry)

Use: The little boy's ambitions were all prosaic. He said he wanted to be an accountant, an auditor or a claims adjustor.

Proscribe (Verb)

Meaning: to outlaw, to prohibit

Use: The young doctor proscribed smoking in the waiting room of his office.

Proselytize (Verb)

Meaning: to convert (someone) from one religion or doctrine to another, to recruit converts to a religion or doctrine

Use: The former Methodist had been proselytized by a Lutheran deacon.

Protagonist (Noun)

Meaning: the leading character in a novel, play or other work, a leader or champion

Use: Martin Luther king - Jr was a protagonist in the long and continuing struggle for racial equality.

Protract (Verb)

Meaning: to prolong

Use: The trial was so protracted that one of the jurors died of old age and another gave birth.

Provident (Adjective)

Meaning: preparing for the future, providing for the future, frugal

Use: The provident father had long ago set aside money for the college educations of each of his children.

Provisional (Adjective)

Meaning: conditional, temporary, tentative

Use: Prashant had been accepted as a provisional member of the club. He wouldn't become a permanent member until the other members had had a chance to see what he was really like.

Proximity (Noun)

Meaning: nearness

Use: I can't stand being in the proximity of a nuclear explosion. The radiation leaves my hair a mess.

Prudent (Adjective)

Meaning: careful, having foresight

Use: Jimmy is a prudent money manager. He doesn't invest heavily in race-horses and he puts only a small part of his savings in the office football pool. Jimmy is the epitome of prudence.

Purported (Adjective)

Meaning: rumored, claimed

Use: The heiress is purported to have been kidnapped by adventurers and buried in a concrete vault beneath the busiest intersection in Times Square.

Putative (Adjective)

Meaning: commonly accepted, supposed, reputed

Use: The putative reason for placing the monument downtown is that nobody had wanted it uptown.

Q

Quadrant (Noun)

Meaning: fourth part of circle

Use: You can use different colour for each quadrant.

Quail (Verb)

Meaning: to tremble with fear

Use: The very word makes many of us quail.

Qualification (Noun)

Meaning: training, ability

Use: That time with him is my qualification to write the book.

Quality (Noun)

Meaning: high degree of goodness

Use: Kindness is a human quality which everyone admires.

Qualify (Verb)

Meaning: to modify or restrict

Use: Susan qualified her praise of Judith by saying that her kind words applied only to Judith's skillful cooking and not to her abhorrent personality. Judith was upset by Susan's qualification.

Qualitative (Adjective)

Meaning: having to do with the quality or qualities of something

Use: If a school achieves a qualitative improvement in attendance, it means that the school is being attended by better students.

Quarrel (Noun)

Meaning: angry, dispute

Use: My brother quarreled with my father.

Quart (Noun)

Meaning: fourth part of gallon

Use: Quart is used in liquid measure.

Quarterly (Adjective)

Meaning: occurring once a quarter

Use: Interest is compounded quarterly.

Quartern (Noun)

Meaning: fourth part of pint

Use: Quartern is used to measure weight.

Quartz (Noun)

Meaning: kind of rock crystal

Use: Quartz is used in manufacturing of glass.

Quaver (Verb)

Meaning: to shake, to tremble

Use: Her voice quavered and she fell silent.

Queen (Noun)

Meaning: wife of king

Use: The king and his queen both were present at ceremony.

Quern (Noun)

Meaning: stone hand-mill for grinding corn

Use: The farmers use quern for their fields.

Querulous (Adjective)

Meaning: complaining; grumbling; whining

Use: Although a query is a question, querulous does not mean questioning.

Quest (Noun)

Meaning: search enquiry

Use: His quest is to find true love.

Questionable (Adjective)

Meaning: doubtful, uncertain

Use: The film is a comedy in highly questionable taste.

Queue (Noun)

Meaning: a line of people waiting for something or to do something

Use: We queued up for tickets.

Quiddity (Noun)

Meaning: essence, quibble

Use: The heart is a quiddity of human body.

Quiet (Adjective)

Meaning: free from noise

Use: He wants some peace and quiet place.

Quilt (Noun)

Meaning: cushion of bed

Use: I use quilt in winters.

Quit (Verb)

Meaning: to abandon

Use: He figured he would quit his job before he was fired.

Quiver (Noun)

Meaning: case for holding arrows

Use: The leaves quivered in the breeze.

Quixote (Noun)

Meaning: fantastically visionary person

Use: His brother is Quixote.

Quixotic (Adjective)

Meaning: romantic or idealistic to a foolish or impractical degree

Use: The political organisation had been powerful force in Washington, but its membership had dwindled and its causes had become increasingly quixotic.

Quadrant (Noun)

Meaning: the area included between such an arc and two radii drawn one to each extremity

Use: The quadrant shaped piece of cake was delicious.

Quadrilateral (Adjective)

Meaning: a plan figure having four sides and consequently four angles

Use: Simple quadrilaterals are either convex or concave.

Quaint (Adjective)

Meaning: attractively old fashioned

Use: Roofs of Nigerian houses are quaint.

Qualification (Noun)

Meaning: an attribute that must be met or complied with and that fits a person for something

Use: Her qualifications for the job are excellent.

Qualify (Verb)

Meaning: prove capable or fit

Use: She was qualified to run the marathon.

Quality (Adjective)

Meaning: a degree or grade of excellence or worth

Use: The quality of students has risen.

Qualm (Noun)

Meaning: sudden attack of disease

Use: Qualms of heartsick agony.

Quantifier (Noun)

Meaning: a word that express a quantity

Use: A lindstrom quantifier is a polyadic quantifier.

Quantity (Noun)

Meaning: an adequate or large amount

Use: He was satisfied with the quantity of cake served to him.

Quarrel (Noun)

Meaning: an angry dispute

Use: They had a quarrel.

Queen (Noun)

Meaning: the wife or widow of King

Meaning: Lakshmibai was the queen of Jhansi.

Question (Noun)

Meaning: the subject matter at question

Use: The question of disease merits serious discussion.

Quick (Adjective)

Meaning: accomplished rapidly and without delay

Use: He was quick to make friends.

Quoin (Noun)

Meaning: external angle of building

Use: Quoin is generally used by printers.

Quotative (Adjective)

Meaning: given to quotation

Use: He is known for his quotative status messages on social networking sites.

Quotient (Noun)

Meaning: number of resulting from division of on quantity

Use: In mathematics, quotient is the result of division.

R

Rabble (Noun)

Meaning: disorderly crowd or mob

Use: They are forced to socialize with the rabble.

Racial (Adjective)

Meaning: pertaining to race

Use: the police is more concern about the protection of national and racial minorities.

Radial (Adjective)

Meaning: of rays or radius

Use: Engineers use radial drilling machine for their work.

Radiance (Noun)

Meaning: brillant luster

Use: The dim bulb cast a soft radiance over his face.

Radiator (Noun)

Meaning: kind of heating apparatus

Use: Radiator is consists of series of pipe.

Radiograph (Noun)

Meaning: photographic pictures taken by x-rays

Use: Doctor suggested him to go for radiograph.

Radius (Noun)

Meaning: straight line from centre of circle to its circumference

Use: They searched within a radius of one mile from the school.

Rafter (Noun)

Meaning: sloping beam to support roof

Use: In ancient time, people used rafter to support house.

Raging (Adjective)

Meaning: furious, violent

Use: He felt a raging thirst.

Railing (Noun)

Meaning: fence of rails

Use: The iron railings of the convent grounds.

Rainbow (Noun)

Meaning: arch of prismatic colours

Use: Chasing the rainbow of overnight success.

Raise (Verb)

Meaning: to lift, to rouse

Use: The car raised a cloud of dust.

Ramble (Verb)

Meaning: to walk for pleasure

Use: Sometimes she tended to ramble.

Ramification (Noun)

Meaning: a consequence, a branching out

Use: The professor found a solution to the problem, but there are many ramifications. Some experts are afraid that he has created more problems than he has solved.

Rancor (Noun)

Meaning: bitter, long-lasting ill will or resentment

Use: The mutual rancor felt by the two nations eventually led to war.

Rancorous (Adjective)

Meaning: spiteful

Use: A series of rancorous disputes.

Ransom (Noun)

Meaning: freeing of prisoner on price

Use: The ransom demand was made by telephone.

Rapacious (Adjective)

Meaning: greedy, plundering, avaricious

Use: Wall Street investment bankers are often accused of being rapacious, but they claim they are performing a valuable economic function.

Rapidly (Noun)

Meaning: swiftness

Use: He was moving rapidly around the room.

Rapture (Noun)

Meaning: ecstasy

Use: His speech was received with rapture by his supporters.

Rascality (Noun)

Meaning: roguery

Use: He behaves like a rascal.

Rational (Adjective)

Meaning: pertaining to reason

Use: There must be a rational explanation for those strange noises.

Rattle (Verb)

Meaning: to clatter

Use: The car was rattling along at top speed.

Ravage (Verb)

Meaning: to lay waste

Use: Enemy soldiers ravaged the village.

Ravenous (Adjective)

Meaning: very hungry

Use: He had moderated his ravenous appetite.

Razor (Noun)

Meaning: instrument used in shaving hair

Use: He cut his face by razor.

Reactionary (Adjective)

Meaning: counteraction, reverse change

Use: Critics viewed him as a reactionary, even a monarchist.

Reality (Noun)

Meaning: actual existence

Use: Fiction and reality were increasingly blurred.

Reanimate (Verb)

Meaning: to revive again

Use: Her dancing reanimates the classical style.

Reasonable (Adjective)

Meaning: rational just and fair

Use: It seems reasonable to expect rapid urban growth.

Reassure (Verb)

Meaning: to give confidence again

Use: The woman was worried about the dangers of taking aspirins, but her doctor reassured her.

Rebuke (Verb)

Meaning: to criticise sharply

Use: The judge rebuked the convicted murderer for chopping up so many people and burying them in the woods.

Rebut (Verb)

Meaning: to contradict, to argue in opposition to, to prove to be false

Use: They all thought I was crazy, but none of them could rebut my argument.

Rebuild (Verb)

Meaning: to build anew

Use: The castle was rebuilt by his great grandson in 1859.

Recalcitrant (Adjective)

Meaning: stubbornly defiant of authority or control, disobedient

Use: The country was in a turmoil, but the recalcitrant dictator refused even to listen to the pleas of the international representatives.

Recant (Verb)

Meaning: to publicly take back and deny (something previously said or believed), to openly confess error

Use: The chagrined scientist recanted his theory that mice originated on the moon. It turned out that he had simply mixed up the results of two separate experiments.

Receipt (Noun)

Meaning: that which is received

Use: Please sign this form to acknowledge the receipt of the money.

Recent (Adjective)

Meaning: having happened

Use: Sales have fallen by more than 75 percent in recent years.

Recharge (Verb)

Meaning: to charge again

Use: He is using your mains electricity to recharge his car battery.

Recitation (Noun)

Meaning: something recited

Use: The letter was a short recitation of their problem.

Reciprocal (Adjective)

Meaning: mutual, shared, interchangeable

Use: The Rochester Club had a reciprocal arrangement with the Duluth Club. Members of either club had full privileges of membership at the other.

Reclusive (Adjective)

Meaning: hermit like, withdrawn from society

Use: Our new neighbours were so reclusive that we did not even meet them until a full year after they had moved in.

Reclaim (Verb)

Meaning: recover wasteland

Use: A wallet has been found and can be reclaimed at the manager's office.

Reclusion (Noun)

Meaning: retirement from society

Use: He is planning for reclusion.

Reconciliation (Noun)

Meaning: state or quality of reconciling

Use: The couple have separated but he wants a reconciliation.

Recreant (Adjective)

Meaning: unfaithful

Use: He is a recreant person.

Recriminate (Verb)

Meaning: to accuse in return

Use: The neighbours recriminate the man of spousal abuse.

Recrimination (Noun)

Meaning: bitter counteraccusation or the act of making a bitter counteraccusation

Use: The courtroom echoed with the recriminations of the convicted defendant as he was taken off to the Penitentiary.

Rectangle (Noun)

Meaning: four sided figure

Use: Rectangle is a four sided polygon.

Reduce (Verb)

Meaning: to bring into order

Use: I must reduce to get into that dress.

Redolent (Adjective)

Meaning: fragrant

Use: The air in autumn is redolent of wood smoke and fallen leaves.

Refute (Verb)

Meaning: to prove to be false, to disprove

Use: His expensive suit and imported shoes clearly refuted his claim that he was poor.

Refinery (Noun)

Meaning: place where metals are refined

Use: I am owner of sugar refinery.

Reformative (Adjective)

Meaning: improving

Use: This factory is reformatting for future.

Refrain (Verb)

Meaning: to hold back

Use: She refrained from making any comment.

Refrigerate (Noun)

Meaning: to cool food for preservation

Use: Refrigerate the dough overnight.

Refuse (Noun)

Meaning: rubbish

Use: I could hardly refuse his invitation.

Regular (Adjective)

Meaning: according to rule

Use: Children are encouraged to make a regular routine.

Reiterate (Verb)

Meaning: to say again, to repeat

Use: The candidate had reiterated his position so many times on the campaign trial that he sometimes even muttered it in his sleep.

Reinstate (Verb)

Meaning: to put in place or office again

Use: He has agreed to reinstate five senior workers.

Relegate (Verb)

Meaning: to banish, to send away

Use: The most junior of the junior executives was relegated to a tiny, windowless office that had once been a broom closet.

Relentless (Adjective)

Meaning: continuous, unstoppable

Use: To relent is to stop or give up. Relentless or unrelenting means not stopping.

Relinquish (Verb)

Meaning: to release or let go of, to surrender, to stop doing

Use: The hungry dog refused to relinquish the enormous beef bone that he had stolen from the butcher's shop.

Remonstrate (Verb)

Meaning: to argue against, to protest, to raise objections

Use: My boss remonstrated with me for telling all the secretaries they could take the rest of the week off.

Renaissance (Noun)

Meaning: a rebirth or revival

Use: The declining neighbourhood underwent a renaissance when a group of investors bought several crumbling tenements and turned them into attractive apartment buildings.

Renounce (Verb)

Meaning: to formally give up or resign, to disown, to have nothing to do with anymore

Use: Despite the pleadings and protestations of her parents, Deborah refused to renounce her love for the leader of the motorcycle gang.

Reparation (Noun)

Meaning: paying back, making amends, compensation

Use: After the accident we sought reparation in court, but out lawyer was not competent and we didn't win a cent.

Repercussion (Noun)

Meaning: a consequence, an indirect effect

Use: One repercussion of the new tax law was that accountants found themselves with a lot of new business.

Replenish (Verb)

Meaning: to fill again, to resupply, to restore

Use: The manager of the hardware store needed to replenish his stock. Quite a few of the shelves were empty.

Replete (Adjective)

Meaning: completely filled, abounding

Use: The once polluted stream was now replete with fish of every description.

Reprehensible (Adjective)

Meaning: worthy of blame or censure

Use: He put the cat in the laundry chute, tied the dog to the chimney and committed several other reprehensible acts.

Reprisal (Noun)

Meaning: a military action undertaken in revenge for another, an act of taking an eye for an eye

Use: Fearing reprisals from the terrorists, the CIA beefed up its security after capturing the terrorist leader.

Reproach (Verb)

Meaning: to scold, usually in disappointment, to blame, to disgrace

Use: My doctor reproached me for gaining twenty pounds after he had advised me to lose fifteen.

Reprove (Verb)

Meaning: to criticise mildly

Use: My wife reproved me for leaving my dirty dish in the sink.

Repudiate (Verb)

Meaning: to reject, to renounce to disown, to have nothing to do with

Use: Hoping to receive a lighter sentence, the convicted gangster repudiated his former connection with the mob.

Requisite (Adjective)

Meaning: required, necessary

Use: Howard bought a hunting rifle and the requisite ammunition.

Resolute (Adjective)

Meaning: determined, firm, unwavering

Use: Uncle Ted was resolute in his decision not to have a good time at our Christmas party. He stood alone in the corner and muttered to himself all night long.

Respite (Noun)

Meaning: a period of rest or relief

Use: We worked without respite from five in the morning until in the afternoon.

Reticent (Adjective)

Meaning: quiet, restrained, reluctant to speak especially about oneself

Use: Luther's natural reticence made him an ideal speaker. His speeches never lasted more than a few minutes.

Revere (Verb)

Meaning: to respect highly, to honour

Use: Piyush made jokes about his younger sister's painting. Piyush's sister was perturbed at his irreverence and began to cry.

Rhetoric (Noun)

Meaning: the art of formal speaking or writing, inflated discourse

Use: A talented public speaker might be said to be skilled in rhetoric.

Rigorous (Adjective)

Meaning: strict, harsh, severe

Use: Our exercise program was rigorous but effective. After just a few months, our eighteen hours of daily exercise had begun to pay off.

Robust (Adjective)

Meaning: strong and healthy, vigorous

Use: The hundred-year-old man was still robust. Every morning he ran several miles down to the ocean and jumped in.

Rogue (Noun)

Meaning: a criminally dishonest person, a scoundrel

Use: A rogue is someone who can't be trusted. It is often used however to characterize a playfully mischievous person.

Rudimentary (Adjective)

Meaning: basic, crude unformed or undeveloped

Use: The boy who had lived with wolves for fifteen years lacked even the most rudimentary social skills.

Ruminate (Verb)

Meaning: to contemplate, to ponder, to mull over

Use: The teacher's comment about the causes of weather set me to ruminate about what a nice day it was and to wishing that I were outside.

Rustic (Adjective)

Meaning: rural, lacking urban comforts or sophistication, primitive

Use: Life in the log cabin was too rustic for Leah. She missed hot showers, cold beer and electricity.

Rusty (Adjective)

Meaning: covered with rust

Use: Her hair was rusty brown.

S

Saccharine (Adjective)

Meaning: sweet, excessively or disgustingly sweet

Use: Saccharin is a calorie-free sweetener. Saccharine means sweet. Except for the spelling, this is one of the easiest to remember words there is. Don't screw up.

Sacrilege (Noun)

Meaning: a violation of something sacred, blasphemy

Use: The minister committed the sacrilege of delivering his sermon while wearing his golf shoes. He didn't want to be late for his tea-off time which was just a few minutes after the scheduled end of the service.

Sacrosanct (Adjective)

Meaning: sacred, held to be inviolable

Use: A church is sacrosanct. So, for Christians, is belief in the divinity of Jesus Christ.

Sagacious (Adjective)

Meaning: discerning, shrewd, keen in judgement, wise

Use: Edgar's decision to move the chickens into the barn turned out to be sagacious; about an hour later, the hailstorm hit.

Salient (Adjective)

Meaning: sticking out, conspicuous, leaping

Use: A salient characteristic is one that leaps right out at you.

Salutary (Adjective)

Meaning: healthful, remedial, curative

Use: Lowered blood pressure is among the salutary effects of exercise.

Sardonic (Adjective)

Meaning: mocking, scornful

Use: Robert's weak attempts at humor were met by nothing but a few scattered pockets of sardonic laughter.

Scintillate (Verb)

Meaning: to sparkle, either literally or figuratively

Use: Stars and diamonds scintillate; so do witty comments, charming personalities and anything else that can be said to sparkle.

Scrupulous (Adjective)

Meaning: strict, careful, hesitant for ethical reasons

Use: We tried to be scrupulous about not dripping paint, but by the time the day was over there was nearly as much paint on the floor as there was on the walls.

Scrutinize (Verb)

Meaning: to examine very carefully

Use: The rocket scientists scrutinized thousands of pages of computer printouts, looking for a clue to why the rocket had exploded.

Sensory (Adjective)

Meaning: having to do with the senses or sensation

Use: Babies enjoy bright colours, moving objects, pleasant sounds and other forms of sensory stimulation.

Sentient (Adjective)

Meaning: able to perceive by the senses, conscious

Use: Human beings are sentient. Rocks are not.

Sequester (Verb)

Meaning: to set or keep apart

Use: The struggling writer sequestered himself in his study for several months, trying to produce the Great American Novel.

Serendipity (Noun)

Meaning: accidental good fortune, discovering good things without looking for them

Use: Something that occurs through serendipity is serendipitous.

Servile (Adjective)

Meaning: submissive and subservient, like a servant

Use: Cat lovers sometimes say that dogs are too servile. They follow their owners everywhere and slobber all over them at every opportunity.

Singular (Adjective)

Meaning: unique, superior, exceptional, strange

Use: Dale had the singular ability to stand on one big toe for several hours at a stretch.

Slander (Verb)

Meaning: to speak badly about someone publicly, to defame, to spread malicious rumour

Use: Jonathan slandered Mr. Periwinkle by telling everyone in school that the principal wore a toupee. Mr. Periwinkle resented this slander. Since he was the principal, he expelled the slanderous student.

Sloth (Noun)

Meaning: laziness, sluggishness

Use: You may have seen a picture of an animal called a sloth. It hangs upside down from tree limbs and is never in a hurry to do anything. To fall into sloth is to act like a sloth.

Sobriety (Noun)

Meaning: the state of being sober, seriousness

Use: A sober person is a person who isn't drunk. A sober person can also be a person who is serious, solemn or not ostentatious. Sobriety means both underunkness and seriousness or solemnity.

Solicitous (Adjective)

Meaning: eager and attentive, often to the point of hovering, anxiously caring or attentive

Use: When the sick movie star sneezed, half a dozen solicitous nurses came rushing into his hospital room.

Solvent (Adjective)

Meaning: not broke or bankrupt, able to pay one's bills

Use: Jerry didn't hope to become a millionaire. All he wanted to do was to remain solvent.

Soporific (Adjective)

Meaning: sleep inducting, extremely boring, very sleepy

Use: The doctor calmed his hysterical patient by injecting him with some sort of soporific medication.

Sordid (Adjective)

Meaning: vile, filthy, squalid

Use: The conspirators plotted their sordid schemes at a series of secret meetings in an abandoned warehouse.

Spawn (Verb)

Meaning: to bring forth, to produce a large number

Use: A best-selling book or blockbuster movie will spawn dozens of imitators.

Specious (Adjective)

Meaning: deceptively plausible or attractive

Use: The river's beauty turned out to be specious. What had looked like churning rapids from a distance was, on closer inspection, some sort of foamy industrial waste.

Sporadic (Adjective)

Meaning: stopping and starting, scattered, occurring in bursts every once in a while

Use: The bathers were made jittery by sporadic gunfire that peppered the beach.

Spurious (Adjective)

Meaning: false, fake

Use: The political candidate attributed his loss to numerous spurious rumors that hounded him throughout his campaign.

Squander (Verb)

Meaning: to waste

Use: Jerry failed to husband his inheritance. Instead, he squandered it on stuffed toys.

Stagnation (Noun)

Meaning: motionlessness, inactivity

Use: The company grew quickly for several years and then fell into stagnation.

Static (Adjective)

Meaning: stationary, not changing or moving

Use: Sales of the new book soared for a few weeks and then became static.

Staunch (Adjective)

Meaning: firmly committed; firmly in favour of; steadfast

Use: A staunch supporter of tax reform would be someone who firmly believes in tax reform.

Steadfast (Adjective)

Meaning: loyal, faithful

Use: Steadfast love is love that never wavers.

Stigmatize (Verb)

Meaning: to brand with disgrace, to set a mark of disgrace upon

Use: Steve's jeans were Lee's instead of Levi's, and this mistake stigmatized him for the rest of his high school career.

Stratum (Noun)

Meaning: a layer, a level

Use: The middle class is one stratum of society.

Stricture (Noun)

Meaning: a restriction, a limitation, a negative criticism

Use: The unfavourable lease placed many strictures on how the building could be used.

Strife (Noun)

Meaning: bitter conflict, discord, a struggle or clash

Use: Marital strife often leads to divorce.

Stringent (Adjective)

Meaning: strict, restrictive

Use: The restaurant's stringent dress code required diners to wear paper hats, army boots and battery-operated twirling bow ties.

Stymie (Verb)

Meaning: to thwart, to get in the way of, to hinder

Use: Stymie is a golfing term. A golfer is stymied when another player's ball lies on the direct path between his or her own ball and the cup.

Subjugate (Verb)

Meaning: to subdue and dominate, to enslave

Use: The tyrant subjugated all the peasants living in the kingdom. Once free, they were now forced to do his bidding.

Sublime (Adjective)

Meaning: awesome, extremely exalted, lofty, majestic

Use: Theodoure was a sublime thinker. After pondering even a difficult problem for just a few minutes, he would invariably arrive at a concise and elegant solution.

Subordinate (Adjective)

Meaning: lower in importance, position, or rank, secondary

Use: A Vice President is subordinate to a President.

Substantive (Adjective)

Meaning: having substance, real' essential, solid, substantial

Use: The Differences between the two theories were not substantive. In fact, the two theories said the same thing with different words.

Subtle (Adjective)

Meaning: not obvious, able to make fine distinctions, ingenious, crafty

Use: Jatin's subtle mind enables him to see past problems that confuse the rest of us.

Subversive (Adjective)

Meaning: corrupting, overthrowing, undermining, insurgent

Use: Sunita's efforts to teach her first-grade students to read were thwarted by that most subversive of inventions that is the television set.

Succinct (Adjective)

Meaning: brief and to the point, concise

Use: We were given so little room in which to write on the examination that we had no choice but to keep our essays succinct.

Succumb (Verb)

Meaning: to yield or submit, to die

Use: I had said I wasn't going to eat anything at the party, but when Ann held the tray of imported chocolates under my nose, I quickly succumbed and ate all of them.

Supercilious (Adjective)

Meaning: haughty, patronizing

Use: The supercilious Rolls-Royce salesman treated us like peasants until we opened our suitcase full of one-hundred-dollar bills.

Superficial (Adjective)

Meaning: on the surface only, shallow, not thorough

Use: Tom had indeed been shot, but the wound was superficial. The bullet had merely creased the tip of his nose.

Superfluous (Adjective)

Meaning: extra, unnecessary, redundant

Use: Andrew's attempt to repair the light bulb was superfluous, since the light bulb had already been repaired.

Surfeit (Noun)

Meaning: excess, an excessive amount, excess or overindulgence in eating or drinking

Use: Thanksgiving meals are usually a surfeit for everyone involved.

Surreptitious (Adjective)

Meaning: sneaky, secret

Use: The baby-sitter mixed herself a surreptitious cocktail as soon as Mr. and Mrs. Rohit had driven away.

Surrogate (Adjective)

Meaning: substitute

Use: A surrogate mother is a woman who bears a child for someone else.

Sycophant (Noun)

Meaning: one who sucks up to others

Use: The French class seemed to be full of sycophants. The students were always bringing apples to the teacher and telling her how nice she looked.

Synthesis (Noun)

Meaning: the combining of parts to form a whole

Use: A hot fudge sundae is the perfect synthesis of hot fudge and vanilla ice cream.

T

Taboo (Noun)

Meaning: prohibition

Use: Cancer is a taboo subject.

Tacit (Adjective)

Meaning: implied, not spoken

Use: There was tacit agreement among the men that women had no business at their weekly poker game.

Taciturn (Adjective)

Meaning: not talkative by nature

Use: The chairman was so taciturn that we often discovered that we had absolutely no idea about what he was thinking.

Tackle (Noun)

Meaning: appliance of ropes

Use: We need to tackle these problems and save people's lives.

Talent (Noun)

Meaning: ancient roman weight

Use: Both her children have a talent for music.

Talkative (Adjective)

Meaning: loquacious

Use: He suddenly became very talkative, his face slightly flushed.

Tambourine (Noun)

Meaning: small drum with loose tingling metal disks

Use: I love to play tambourine.

Tamper (Verb)

Meaning: to make unauthorized change in document

Use: Don't tamper with my feelings.

Tangential (Adjective)

Meaning: only superficially related to the matter at hand, not especially relevant, peripheral

Use: The mayor's speech bore only a tangential relationship to the topic that had been announced.

Tangible (Adjective)

Meaning: touchable, palpable

Use: A mountain of cigarette butts was the only tangible evidence that Luther had been in our house.

Tantamount (Adjective)

Meaning: equivalent to

Use: Waving a banner for the visiting team at that football game would be tantamount to committing suicide. The home-team fans would tear you apart in a minute.

Taste (Verb)

Meaning: to try or perceive by tongue

Use: She shows good taste in clothes.

Tautological (Adjective)

Meaning: redundant, circular

Use: When everyone has a camera, cameras will be universal is a tautological statement, because everyone having a camera and cameras being universal mean the same thing.

Tavern (Noun)

Meaning: public alehouse

Use: The travelers stopped at a tavern for a meal and a mug of ale.

Teach (Verb)

Meaning: to give knowledge

Use: She teaches English.

Technical (Adjective)

Meaning: pertaining to technique

Use: I hadn't realised how technical our language was.

Tedious (Adjective)

Meaning: tiresome

Use The tedious business of line-by-line programming.

Temerity (Noun)

Meaning: boldness, recklessness, audacity

Use: Our waiter at the restaurant had the temerity to tell me that he thought that my table manners were atrocious.

Temperate (Adjective)

Meaning: mild, moderate, restrained

Use: Our climate is temperate during the spring and fall but very nearly unbearable during the summer and winter.

Tenable (Adjective)

Meaning: defensible, as in one's position in an argument, capable of being argued successfully, valid

Use: Members of the Flat Earth Society continue to argue that the earth is flat, although even children dismiss their arguments as not tenable.

Terse (Adjective)

Meaning: using no unnecessary words, succinct

Use: The new recording secretary's minutes were so terse that they were occasionally cryptic.

Terminate (Verb)

Meaning: to bring to end

Use: His contract terminates at the end of the season.

Terrific (Adjective)

Meaning: dreadful

Use: There was a terrific bang and a great cloud of smoke.

Textile (Adjective)

Meaning: pertaining to weaving

Use: He is the king of textile industry.

Theology (Noun)

Meaning: the study of god or religion

Use: Rakesh was a paradox. He was an atheist yet he passionately studied theology.

Tirade (Noun)

Meaning: prolonged, bitter speech

Use: The Principal launched into a tirade against imitation cheese on the school lunch menu.

Torpor (Noun)

Meaning: sluggishness, inactivity, apathy

Use: The math teacher tried to reduce the torpor of his students by setting off a few firecrackers on his desk, but the students scarcely blinked.

Transient (Adjective)

Meaning: not staying for a long time, temporary

Use: The child's smile was transient. It disappeared as soon as the candy bar was gone.

Transparent (Adjective)

Meaning: able to be seen through

Use: The meaning of their actions is transparent.

Treat (Verb)

Meaning: to behave towards

Use: He took them to the theatre as a treat.

Trepidation (Noun)

Meaning: fear, apprehension, nervous trembling

Use: The nursery school students were filled with trepidation when they saw the other children in their class dressed in their Halloween costumes.

Truculent (Adjective)

Meaning: fierce, cruel

Use: She turned from truculent to silent teenager.

Trust (Noun)

Meaning: firm belief

Use: The companies formed a trust.

Tumult (Noun)

Meaning: uproar, great confusion

Use: The crowd gave him a tumultuous welcome.

Turnip (Noun)

Meaning: large round edible root

Use: Would you like some turnips?

Typhoon(Noun)

Meaning: violent hurricane

Use: They were caught in a typhoon in the china seas.

Typist (Noun)

Meaning: one who prints typewriter

Use: She is working as a typist in MNC.

Tzar (Noun)

Meaning: title

Use: Tzar is another name of ruler.

U

Ubiquitous (Adjective)

Meaning: being everywhere at the same time

Use: Personal computers, once a rarity, have become ubiquitous.

Udometer (Noun)

Meaning: rain-gauge

Use: Udometer is used to measure the quantity of precipitation.

Ulster (Noun)

Meaning: long loose over coat

Use: Ulster is made from rugged fabric.

Umbrageous (Adjective)

Meaning: shady

Use: He has umbrageous figure on the wall.

Unanimity (Noun)

Meaning: agreement of opinion

Use: All decisions would require unanimity.

Unburden (Verb)

Meaning: to relax

Use: He had to unburden his soul to somebody.

Unconscionable (Adjective)

Meaning: not controlled by conscience, unscrupulous

Use: Leaving a small child unattended all day long is an unconscionable act.

Unctuous (Adjective)

Meaning: oily, both literally and figuratively, insincere

Use: Salad oil is literally unctuous. A used-car salesman might be figuratively unctuous that he is oily in the sense of being slick, sleazy and insincere.

Underbrush (Noun)

Meaning: small trees in forest

Use: There are number of underbrush in rainy forest.

Understanding (Noun)

Meaning: ability to understand

Use: we would like to thank them for their patience and understanding.

Undulation (Verb)

Meaning: wavy motion

Use: The sea is in undulation mood.

Unicorn (Noun)

Meaning: act of uniting

Use: A horse with a single straight horn is a symbol of unicorn.

Uniform (Adjective)

Meaning: consistent, unchanging, the same for everyone

Use: Traffic laws are similar from one state to the next, but they aren't uniform. Each state has its own variations.

Unite (Verb)

Meaning: to join together or to become one

Use: They have agreed to unite their efforts to bring peace.

Universal (Adjective)

Meaning: for all

Use: The discovery of literature has as yet only partially penetrated the universal consciousness.

Unmitigated (Adjective)

Meaning: not softened

Use: A senior policeman had called him an unmitigated liar.

Unscrew (Verb)

Meaning: to pull out screw from

Use: Can you unscrew this lid?

Unstitch (Verb)

Meaning: to open stitches

Use: I want to unstitch all this old suit pieces.

Unremitting (Adjective)

Meaning: unceasing, unabated, relentless

Use: Superman waged an unremitting battle against evildoers everywhere.

Unwitting (Adjective)

Meaning: unintentional, ignorant, not aware

Use: When Leo agreed to hold open the door of the bank, he became an unwitting accomplice to the bank robbery.

Uphold (Verb)

Meaning: to Support

Use: The old traditions are still upheld in this village.

Upholster (Verb)

Meaning: to furnish with floor carpet

Use: He upholstered the chair.

Upland (Noun)

Meaning: elevated ground

Use: They lived in upland area.

Uprise (Verb)

Meaning: to arise

Use: The sun is uprising towards the sky.

Uproarious (Adjective)

Meaning: tumultuous

Use: He had spent several uproarious evenings at the Embassy club.

Upshot (Noun)

Meaning: final result

Use: So the upshot is we are going for lunch on Friday.

Upward (Adjective)

Meaning: towards higher place

Use: She started once again on the steep upward climb.

Urbane (Adjective)

Meaning: poised, sophisticated, refined

Use: The British count was witty and urbane. All the hosts and hostesses wanted to have him at their parties.

Urge (Verb)

Meaning: to drive forcibly

Use: He had an urge to open a shop of his own.

Usage (Noun)

Meaning: practice

Use: Parts of the motor wore out because of constant usage.

Useless (Adjective)

Meaning: of no use

Use: He realised that their money was useless in this country.

Usually (Adverb)

Meaning: ordinarly

Use: The best information about hotels usually comes from friends.

Usurp (Verb)

Meaning: to seize wrongfully

Use: The children believed that their mother's new boyfriend had usurped their real father's rightful place in their family.

Utopia (Noun)

Meaning: an ideal society

Use: A country where nobody had to work and Monody Night Football was on television every night would be Quentin's idea of utopia.

Utilitarian (Adjective)

Meaning: stressing usefulness or utility above all other qualities, pragmatic

Use: Jason's interior-decorating philosophy was strictly utilitarian. If an object wasn't genuinely useful, he didn't want it in his home.

Utensil (Noun)

Meaning: domestic tool or vessel

Use: The technique uses a single utensil to cook and serve.

Utilize (Verb)

Meaning: to make use of

Use: Sound engineers utilize a range of techniques.

Utterly (Adverb)

Meaning: completely

Use: The new laws coming in are utterly ridiculous.

Uzbeg (Noun)

Meaning: race of people living in central Asia

Use: The Turkish language is spoken by many Uzbeg.

V

Vacation (Noun)

Meaning: holiday

Use: She went to Japan for vacation.

Vaccination (Noun)

Meaning: act of vaccinating

Use: Vaccination is important to protect against disease.

Vacillate (Verb)

Meaning: to be indecisive, to waver

Use: Tittoo vacillated about buying a new car. He couldn't decide whether to get one or not.

Vagrant (Adjective)

Meaning: wandering

Use: Vagrancy is a crime in some countries.

Vain (Adjective)

Meaning: unsubstantial

Use: They worked all night in a vain attempt to finish on schedule.

Valid (Adjective)

Meaning: strong

Use: For foreign holidays you will need a valid passport.

Valorous (Adjective)

Meaning: courageous

Use: She is a valorous woman.

Vanguard (Noun)

Meaning: front part of fighting army

Use: Students have been in the vanguard of revolutionary change in India.

Vaporize (Verb)

Meaning: to convert into vapour

Use: Water is vaporizing because of heat.

Vapid (Adjective)

Meaning: without liveliness, dull, spiritless

Use: The novelist's prose was so vapid that Mary couldn't get beyond the first page.

Variable (Adjective)

Meaning: changeable

Use: Weather conditions are variable and change from day to day.

Vehement (Adjective)

Meaning: intense, forceful, violent

Use: Shaking his fist and stamping his foot, Gerry was vehement in his denial.

Velocity (Noun)

Meaning: swiftness

Use: The velocity at which the planets orbit.

Venal (Adjective)

Meaning: capable of being bribed, willing to do anything for money, corrupt

Use: The venal judge reversed his favourable ruling when the defendant refused to make good on his promised bribe.

Venerate (Verb)

Meaning: to revere, to treat as something holy especially because of great age

Use: Lester venerated his grandfather. He worshipped the very ground the old man limped on.

Veneration (Noun)

Meaning: high reverence

Use: The veneration of man has been misdirected.

Ventilate (Verb)

Meaning: air to pass through

Use: Churchill was held in veneration in his lifetime.

Veracity (Noun)

Meaning: truthfulness

Use: The veracity of young George Washington is legendary, but it may be apocryphal.

Verification (Noun)

Meaning: act of confirming

Use: There is no independent verification of this story.

Version (Noun)

Meaning: translation

Use: She went public with her version of events.

Verbose (Adjective)

Meaning: using too many words, not succinct, circumlocutory

Use: Someone who is verbose uses too many words when fewer words would suffice.

Verisimilitude (Noun)

Meaning: similarity to reality, the appearance of truth, looking like the real thing

Use: They used pinecones and old truck tires to make statues of Hollywood celebrities that were remarkable for their verisimilitude.

Vernacular (Noun)

Meaning: everyday speech, slang, idiom

Use: Our teacher said that we should save our vernacular for the street. In the classroom we should use proper grammar.

Vestige (Noun)

Meaning: a remaining bit of something, a last trace

Use: An old uniform and a tattered scrapbook were the only vestiges of the old man's career as a professional athlete.

Vex (Verb)

Meaning: to annoy, to pester, to confuse

Use: Margaret vexed me by poking me with a long and sharp stick.

Viable (Adjective)

Meaning: capable of living, workable

Use: When a doctor says that a patient is no longer viable, it's time to begin planning a funeral.

Vicarious (Adjective)

Meaning: experienced, performed or suffered through someone else, living through the experiences of another as though they were one's own experiences

Use: To take vicarious pleasure in someone else's success is to enjoy that person's success as though it were your own.

Vicissitude (Noun)

Meaning: upheaval, natural change, change is fortune

Use: The vicissitudes of the stock market were too much for Penny. She decided to look for a job that would stay the same from one day to the next.

Vilify (Verb)

Meaning: to say vile things about, to defame

Use: The teacher was reprimanded for vilifying the slow student in front of the rest of the class.

Vindicate (Verb)

Meaning: to clear from all blame or suspicion, to justify

Use: Tony, having been accused of stealing money from the cash register, was vindicated when the store manager counted the money again and found that none was missing after all.

Vindictive (Adjective)

Meaning: seeking revenge

Use: Samantha's vindictive ex-husband drove all the way across the country just to punch her in the nose.

Virtuoso (Noun)

Meaning: a masterful musician, a masterful practitioner in some other filed

Use: The concert audience fell silent when the virtuoso stepped forward to play the sonata on his electric banjo.

Virulent (Adjective)

Meaning: extremely poisonous, malignant, full of hate

Use: The snake was a member of particularly virulent breed. Its bite could kill an elephant.

Visionary (Noun)

Meaning: a dreamer, someone with impractical goals or ideas about the future

Use: The candidate was a visionary. He had a lot of big ideas but no realistic plan for putting them into practice.

Vitiate (Verb)

Meaning: to make impure, to pollute

Use: For years a zealous group of individuals has campaigned against the use of fluoride in water, claiming that it has vitiated our bodies as well as our morals.

Vitriolic (Adjective)

Meaning: caustic, full of bitterness

Use: The review of the new book was so vitriolic that we all wondered whether the reviewer had some personal grudge against the author.

Vocation (Noun)

Meaning: an occupation, a job

Use: Your vocation is what you do for a living.

Vociferous (Adjective)

Meaning: loud, noisy

Use: Randy often becomes vociferous during arguments. He doesn't know what he believes but he states it loudly nevertheless.

Volatile (Adjective)

Meaning: quick to evaporate, highly unstable, explosive

Use: A volatile liquid is one that evaporates readily.

Volition (Noun)

Meaning: a will, conscious choice

Use: Insects, lacking volition, simply aren't as interesting as humans are.

Vocalize (Verb)

Meaning: to form into voice

Use: She needs to vocalize her issues or else she'll be ruined.

Volunteer (Noun)

Meaning: one who joins welfare

Use: She volunteered for the dangerous job.

Vulpine (Adjective)

Meaning: pertaining to foxes

Use: Vulpine is a cunning animal.

Voyage (Noun)

Meaning: journey by sea

Use: They voyaged for many months.

W

Waddle (Verb)

Meaning: to walk with short steps

Use: A fat woman waddling down the street.

Wagtail (Noun)

Meaning: kind of bird

Use: Wagtile is an oscine bird.

Wanton (Adjective)

Meaning: malicious, unjustifiable, unprovoked, egregious

Use: Terrorists commit wanton acts on a helpless populace to make their point.

Warning (Noun)

Meaning: caution

Use: Pain can act as a warning signal that something is wrong.

Warrior (Noun)

Meaning: champion, soldier

Use: Neighbourhood warriors fighting against developers.

Wasteful (Adjective)

Meaning: causing waste

Use: Don't do the wasteful consumption of fuel.

Waterish (Adjective)

Meaning: thin as water

Use: His eyes become waterish.

Wave (Noun)

Meaning: swell on surface of water

Use: The blast wave crushed his breath.

Way (Noun)

Meaning: road, direction

Use: He went out of his way to help us.

Wealthy (Adjective)

Meaning: rich

Use: He is a wealthy businessman.

Weather (Noun)

Meaning: day to day condition of atmosphere

Use: In India weather changes after every two months.

Wedge (Noun)

Meaning: piece of metal or wood

Use: His nomination drove a wedge into party unity.

Willful (Adjective)

Meaning: deliberate, obstinate, insistent on having one's way

Use: The mother insisted that the killing committed by her son had not been willful, but the jury apparently believed that he had known what he was doing.

Wistful (Adjective)

Meaning: yearning, sadly longing

Use: I felt wistful when I saw John's fancy new Car. I wished that I had enough money to buy one for myself.

Withstand (Verb)

Meaning: to oppose

Use: A politician has to be able to withstand criticism from the press.

Wizard (Noun)

Meaning: magician

Use: A mathematical wizard at Harvard university.

Workmanship (Noun)

Meaning: skill of workman

Use: He is a carpenter who prided himself on the quality of his workmanship.

Worshipper (Noun)

Meaning: devotee, one who worships

Use: Worshipper never worships with greed.

Wrangler (Noun)

Meaning: one who disputes

Use: Everywhere he plays a role of wrangler.

Wrest (Verb)

Meaning: to twist

Use: He has been trying to wrest control from the central government.

Wristlet (Noun)

Meaning: bracelet

Use: He presents me a wristlet.

Writer (Noun)

Meaning: author

Use: Rohan wants to become a story writer.

Wrong (Adjective)

Meaning: not right

Use: We think there's something wrong with the computer.

Wynd (Noun)

Meaning: narrow lane

Use: This valley is full of wynds.

X

Xanthic (Adjective)

Meaning: fair haired

Use: The xanthic nature of this flower attracted all the children.

Xanadu (Noun)

Meaning: an exotic, luxurious place

Use: Million – square – footed xanadu meadowlands one had smashed suddenly so popular of Infinite capacity.

Xanax (Noun)

Meaning: a pharmaceutical drug that is used to treat depression and anxiety

Use: Excess amount of Xanax drug slowed down the activities of nervous system.

Xanthic (Noun)

Meaning: yellowish in colour; having to do with the compound

Use: The salts of any class of organic sulphur – containing acids are the xanthates.

Xanthein (Noun)

Meaning: yellow colouring matter of flower

Use: The colour of the walls is xanthein.

Xebec

Meaning: a xebec is a special three-masted sailing ship used in the Mediterranean

Use: Xebecs are formerly armed and used by corsairs.

Xenolith (Noun)

Meaning: a fragment of a rock embedded inside another rock

Use: Xenolith of granite indicates the near proximity of granite at depth.

Xenon

Meaning: scientists call xenon one of the noble gases. It's odourless, colourless, and found in very small quantities in the Earth's atmosphere

Use: A technique has been available for assessing cerebrals blood flow on CT machines using the inert gas xenon since the 1970s.

Xeric (Adjective)

Meaning: dry or desert like conditions; having very little moisture

Use: Xeric monocotyledonous mats on inselbergs in West Africa and Atlantic central Africa.

Xerography (Noun)

Meaning: the word for a process to copy documents is xerography

Use: In 1937, the process called Xerography was invented by American Law student Chester Carlson.

Xerox (Verb)

Meaning: xerox is the patented process for copying documents, and the name of a corporation. The word Xerox should never be used as a synonym for photocopying a document

Use: In my office, we have seven Xerox machines.

Xhosa

Meaning: Xhosa is the name of the Bantu language, and a name for a member of the Bantu people of South Africa.

Use: We need a translator of xhosa language to write few books.

Xylem (Noun)

Meaning: botanists describe the tubes within the stems of woody plants as xylem. The xylem conducts fluids up the plant, while phloem brings the fluids down

Use: The cells which make up a xylem vessel are dead cells.

Xylograph (Noun)

Meaning: a wood engraving

Use: The coloured xylograph has a single – leaf prints from about 1450.

Xyloid (Adjective)

Meaning: resembling wood; woody

Use: We don't have any matching xyloid yet for this process.

Xylophone (Noun)

Meaning: a percussion instrument with wood or metal tubes struck with hammers

Use: He can't keep away from the amazing wooden xylophone.

XML(Noun)

Meaning: a computer language abbreviation for extensible markup language

Use: We use XML language in computers.

Y

Yam (Noun)

Meaning: any of numerous chiefly tropical vines of the genus Dioscorea, many of which have edible tuberous root

Use: Tom Yam is a hot and sour Thai soup.

Yank (Noun)

Meaning: someone from the Northern United States

Use: Canadian about a political party that plays them. to voters' anti-Americanism but swoons over the first big- name Yank who will acknowledge them.

Yardstick (Noun)

Meaning: a graduated measuring stick one yard in length

Use: Tolstoy wrote a long, strange story called Yardstick, the name of the horse and the most imaginative original knowing horse narrative in literary history.

Yarn (Noun)

Meaning: thread made of natural or synthetic fibers and used for knitting and weaving

Use: These are two long length sweater patterns with a thick cable and ribbed design knitted in aran weight yarn.

Yawn (Verb)

Meaning: to stretch the mouth wide and take a deep breath when tired or bored

Use: He yawned and fell asleep.

Year (Noun)

Meaning: a period of approximately the duration of a calendar year

Use: We were married a year ago.

Yeast (Noun)

Meaning: an agent of ferment or activity

Use: Political agitators who are the yeast of revolution.

Yellow (Noun)

Meaning: the hue of that portion of the visible spectrum lying between orange and green, evoked in the human observer by radiant energy with wave lengths of approximately 570 to 590 nanometers

Use: The walls have been painted bright yellow.

Yes (Adverb)

Meaning: used to express affirmation, agreement, positive, confirmation or consent

Use: Yes, that is true; Yes, you may go.

Yesterday (Noun)

Meaning: the day before the present day; also the time in the past, especially the recent past

Use: Yesterday was a tiring day.

Yet (Adverb)

Meaning: up to specified time; thus far

Use: The end had not come yet.

Yield (Verb)

Meaning: to give forth by or as if by a natural process

Use: He yielded to their consistent demands.

Yoga (Noun)

Meaning: any of several systems of physical exercises on a Hindu system of philosophy and meditation

Use: Yoga is the best medicine for health.

You (Pronoun)

Meaning: used to refer to the one or ones being addressed

Use: I'll lend you the book. You shouldn't work so hard.

Youth (Noun)

Meaning: the condition or quality of being young

Use: Youth everywhere is rising in revolt.

Yo-yo (Noun)

Meaning: a toy consisting of a flattened spool that is reeled up and down on a string by motions of the hand

Use: Small kids like Yo-yo toy.

Yummy (Adjective)

Meaning: very pleasing to the taste or smell, delicious

Use: Butterscotch ice cream is yummy.

Z

Zap (Verb)

Meaning: to add a sudden infusion of energy

Use: Just the thing to Zap up your spring wardrobe.

Zealous (Adjective)

Meaning: enthusiastically devoted to something, fervent

Use: The zealous young policeman made so many arrests that the city jail soon became overcrowded.

Zebra (Noun)

Meaning: any of several swift, wild, horselike African mammals of the genus Equus, having distinctive overall markings of alternating white and black or brown stripes

Use: We have to stand apart from the crowd, just like the red striped zebra.

Zest (Noun)

Meaning: the outermost part of the rind of an orange, lemon or other citrus fruits used for flavouring

Use: For the curd, put the zest and sugar in a food processor and pulse until combined and the zest is broken down.

Zigzag (Noun)

Meaning: a line or course that proceeds by sharp turns in alternating directions

Use: Shooting at them on the zigzag is iffy at best, but hard to resist.

Zinc (Noun)

Meaning: a bluish-white, lustrous metallic element that is brittle at room temperature but malleable with heating

Use: The roof is clad in zinc and is cut and folded cleanly to focus views out to the harbor and diagonally to the trees, while at the same time providing a sense of privacy.

ZIP CODE (Noun)

Meaning: a postal code, especially for addresses served by the postal services consisting of alphabets or numbers

Use: In some countries, Zipcodes are alpha numeric.

Zipper (Noun)

Meaning: a fastening device consisting of parallel rows of metal, plastic or nylon teeth on adjacent edges of an opening that are interlocked by a sliding tab

Use: Don't agree with everything you say, but the fish with a zipper is the best comeback I've heard in years.

Zodiac (Noun)

Meaning: in astrology, this band divided into 12 equal parts called signs, each 30 degree wide, bearing the name of a constellation for which it was originally named but with which it no longer coincides owing to the precession of the equinoxes

Use: Leo: Anything really difficult this week will happen when The King of the Zodiac is not present. – Horoscope of this week.

Zone (Noun)

Meaning: an area or a region distinguished from adjacent parts by a distinctive feature or characteristic

Use: Zone is still what we do, but we're going to complement it.

Zoo (Noun)

Meaning: a park or institution in which living animals are kept and usually exhibited to the public

Use: Kids enjoyed a visit to the zoo where they saw different animals.

Zoological (Adjective)

Meaning: of or relating to animal life

Use: Among the different animals in Zoo, they have zoological institution that entrust them with some rare species and they transport all sorts of unique animals.

Zoologist (Noun)

Meaning: a person who studies zoology

Use: The Log-Book of a fisherman and Zoologist by Frank Buckland 1891 makes for an interesting read.

Zoology (Noun)

Meaning: the science of animals

Use: She received her Ph.D in Zoology from the University of London.

Zucchini (Noun)

Meaning: a variety of squash having an elongated shape and a smooth, thin dark green rind

Use: Esther, grilling the zucchini is a fabulous idea — it's my favourite way to make zucchini.

□□□